Urban Enclaves
Identity and Place in America

Contemporary Social Issues

George Ritzer, Series Editor

Forthcoming:

Contemporary Social Issues
Series Editor: George Ritzer, University of Maryland

Urban Enclaves
Identity and Place in America

Mark Abrahamson

University of Connecticut

St. Martin's Press
New York

Editor: Sabra Scribner
Manager, publishing services: Emily Berleth
Packaging project editor: Kalea Chapman
Production supervisor: Joe Ford
Art director: Lucy Krikorian
Cover design: Rod Hernandez
Cover photo: Comstock, Inc.

Manufactured in the United States of America.

0 9 8 7
f e d c b

For information, write:
St. Martin's Press, Inc.
175 Fifth Avenue
New York, NY 10010

ISBN: 0-312-11499-0 (softcover)
ISBN: 0-312-12794-4 (hardcover)

Abrahamson, Mark
Urban enclaves : identity and place in America / Mark Abrahamson.
p. cm. — (Contemporary social issues)
Includes bibliographical references and index.
ISBN 0-312-12794-4 (hardcover)
1. Ethnic neighborhoods—United States. 2. United States—Ethnic relations.
3. United States—Race relations. I. Title. II. Series: Contemporary social issues (New York, N.Y.)
E184.A1A24 1996
305.8′00973—dc20

95-17439
CIP

Contents

Foreword

As we move toward the close of the twentieth century, we confront a seemingly endless array of pressing social issues: crime, urban decay, inequality, ecological threats, rampant consumerism, war, AIDS, inadequate health care, national and personal debt, and many more. Although such problems are regularly dealt with in newspapers, magazines, and trade books and on radio and television, such popular treatment has severe limitations. By examining these issues systematically through the lens of sociology, we can gain greater insight into them and be better able to deal with them. It is to this end that St. Martin's Press has created this series on contemporary social issues.

Each book in the series will cast a new and distinctive light on a familiar social issue, while challenging the conventional view, which may obscure as much as it clarifies. Phenomena that seem disparate and unrelated will be shown to have many commonalities and to reflect a major, but largely unrecognized, trend within the larger society. Or a systematic comparative investigation will demonstrate the existence of social causes or consequences that are overlooked by other types of analysis. In uncovering such realities the books in this series will be much more than intellectual exercises; they will have powerful practical implications for our lives and for the structure of society.

At another level, this series will fill a void in book publishing. There is certainly no shortage of academic titles, but those books tend to be introductory texts for undergraduates or advanced monographs for professional scholars. Missing are broadly accessible, issue-oriented books appropriate for all students (and for general readers). The books in this series will occupy that niche somewhere between popular trade books and monographs. Like trade books, they will deal with important and interesting social issues, be well written, and as jargon free as possible. However, they will be more rigorous than trade books in meeting academic standards for writing and research. Although they are not textbooks, they will often explore topics covered in basic textbooks and therefore will be easily integrated into the curriculum of sociology and other disciplines.

Each of the books in the St. Martin's series "Contemporary Social Issues" is a new and distinctive piece of work. I believe that students, serious general readers, and professors will all find the books to be informative, interesting, thought provoking, and exciting.

George Ritzer, Editor

Preface

Enclaves have always been a part of American cities. In the last twenty years or so, I have been especially fascinated by the growth of self-contained communities composed of new (Asian and Hispanic) immigrants, and of religious and life-style groups. Various books, journal and magazine articles, and presentations at professional meetings have attempted to describe various enclaves, with interesting but limited results because almost all confined themselves to a particular enclave or, at best, to a single type of enclave.

This book is a product of my efforts to compare different types of enclaves; its organization and major thrusts mirror the development of my thought. I first wrestled with definitions of enclaves and related concepts. It was important, I concluded, to combine attachment to a place with people's identities. In Chapter One I try to bring together all the perspectives that seem important in deciding whether a group of people in a particular site constitute an enclave, a near-enclave, or something else entirely.

To make generalization possible, now or later, I thought it necessary to look at a wide assortment of enclaves; the more diverse the better. I "sampled" enclaves that were based on different types of shared identities, and those from different historical periods and in different parts of the country. Within each of Chapters Two through Eight, my first objective is to describe a particular enclave in a way that makes it "real" to the reader, and my second is to compare it with others of the same type in order to clarify the ways in which the enclave of primary focus is an exemplar of a genre. In the final chapter, I try to view enclaves of all types in a larger societal context. I fear that I have been more successful in describing diverse enclaves than in generalizing about them, but I console myself with the hope that others will find what I have done to be helpful.

There are a number of people who have been especially helpful and warrant acknowledgment at this time. George Ritzer, friend of long standing and series editor, prodded me to sit down at the keyboard again while I was making a sometimes difficult transition from an administrative to an academic position. It helped and I am indebted. St. Martin's Sociology Editor, Sabra Scribner, has been wonderful to work with. She has been an uncommonly helpful editor. I would also like to thank the following people who reviewed the manuscript for St. Martin's Press: George Arquitt, Oklahoma State University; Tiffany Hogan, University of Florida; Stanley Schultz, University of Wisconsin-Madison; Kenrick Thompson, Northern Michigan University; and Eugene Uyeki, Case Western Reserve University. My wife, Marlene, has done much to make this book a reality, commenting on the manuscript and providing the encouragement that actually made it very easy to keep writing.

1

An Overview

Robert Park, a pioneering urban theorist, once described cities as comprising "a mosaic of little worlds that touch but do not interpenetrate."[1] With a bit of elaboration, Park's description fit most large American cities, not only when he first offered it in 1925, but even today. He was primarily calling attention to the fact that various types of people tend to seek out others like themselves and live close together. Located within these distinctive clusters are specialized commercial enterprises and institutions that support the inhabitants' special ways of life. Examples include grocery stores and restaurants that offer food from people's countries of origin; bars, theaters, and night clubs that cater to particular life-styles and interests; and churches of various denominations, synagogues, and mosques.

Each distinctive group, along with its stores and institutions, occupies a geographic area that becomes intimately associated with the group. Through this linkage, areas acquire symbolic qualities that include their place names and social histories. Each place, both as a geographic entity and as a space with social meaning, also tends to be an object of residents' attachments and an important component of their identities. For example, people living in Little Italy or Chinatown think of themselves as Italian or Chinese, but their place of residence is also a prominent part of their self-concepts. Because many relationships tend to revolve around place of residence, Park concluded that people who live in "little worlds" have their most meaningful relationships with those who cohabit their worlds.

The little worlds Park wrote about, when given the above clarifications, come very close to constituting what we will refer to as *enclaves*. To use the term *enclave* in this manner requires some broadening of its customary referents, though. In prior writings it has most frequently been used to refer to racial or ethnic minorities living in economically self-contained ghettos such as Miami's Little Havana.[2] We will retain this usage, and in addition we shall use *enclave* to refer to concentrations of residents who do not have the same ethnic or minority status in the conventional sense, but who share

1

a significant commonality based on wealth, life-style, or a combination of these attributes. The Castro district of San Francisco, for example, includes a residential area largely populated by men who are openly gay. This distinctive group supports a complete array of gay-oriented commercial and institutional activities: gay nightclubs and bars, bookstores, churches, and therapists and clinics specializing in the treatment of gay patients, and so on. In San Francisco, the *Gay Yellow Pages* directory is comparable to the *Chinese Yellow Pages* or *Hispanic Yellow Pages*.[3] The Castro as a place is also an important part of residents' identities. Therefore, this community based on life-style should also be regarded as an enclave.

Our use of the term *enclave* will expand on prior usages in two other ways. First, enclaves have traditionally been viewed as existing only in inner cities. As the metropolitan areas around cities have grown in size and complexity, however, communities with all the features of enclaves have formed in otherwise conventional suburbs. They should be regarded as enclaves despite not being located in central cities. Second, past studies have emphasized the commercial self-sufficiency of enclaves to differentiate them from ghettos, which involve only distinctive population concentrations. Although we will regard the commercial dimension as an important component in defining enclaves, in addition we will place a similar emphasis on institutional development in the noneconomic realm. An enclave will typically possess a reasonably high degree of commercial as well as institutional development. In special circumstances, however, either may be sufficient to warrant calling a place an enclave.

Both the suburban and noneconomic features described in the preceding paragraph are illustrated by "Kiryas Joel," the Village of Joel. In 1977, several thousand Hasidic Jews moved from Brooklyn to Orange County, New York, about forty miles northwest of the city. They were seeking a place where they could follow, without compromise, the teachings of their religious leader, Rebbe Joel Teitelbaum. It was for him they named the new community Kiryas Joel. In homes and in the religious schools that all the Hasidic youngsters attend, Yiddish and Hebrew are the main languages. English is a "second" language, and most youngsters in the village know little about the world outside. The village now contains 10,000–12,000 people, and most of the adults who work are employed outside of the village, either in New York City or in an industrial park about twenty miles away. Some of the residents operate local businesses (such as kosher food stores) that meet the Hasidic residents' distinctive needs. However, what most makes this suburban community an enclave lies outside the economic realm. Its residents share an identity, a commitment to a place, and a way of life in which religious institutions provide the central organizing theme.[4]

As all of the preceding examples imply, an enclave involves a special relationship between a distinctive group of people and a place. Thus, an enclave has some characteristics of a subculture, in which a group of people shares common traditions and values that are ordinarily maintained by a high rate of interaction within the group. All subcultures do not have the requisite place tie to be classified as enclaves, however, and all groups with place ties do not necessarily qualify as subcultures.

Contemporary Gypsies provide an example of a subculture without a place tie. There are some sizeable concentrations of Gypsies in major cities of the United States; as many as 15,000 have been estimated to live at least part of the year in Los Angeles neighborhoods. However, as their name itself has come to signify, the Gypsies are highly mobile. They migrate across the country, working in traveling carnivals, sometimes sealing driveways, telling fortunes, working temporarily in automobile repair shops. They undertake much of this travel in order to visit friends and family, especially to celebrate Gypsy holidays. Their high rate of within-group interaction has enabled them to perpetuate shared values and a distinctive way of life, but this has not been accompanied by the establishment of ties to a place. For this reason, the Gypsies provide an example of a subculture but not of an enclave.[5]

On the other hand, many of the homeless in Austin, Texas, provide an example of a group with a local place tie, but not the shared values and meaningful interactions ordinarily associated with a subculture. According to sociologists David A. Snow and Leon Anderson, who spent two years studying the homeless in Austin, a large number of these homeless people remain in Austin, spending years together on the streets in more or less defined areas and sleeping and eating in shelters like the Salvation Army's. Given their common human needs and lack of resources with which to meet them, most of these homeless people tend to respond similarly to similar circumstances, though they have few meaningful relationships with others. Furthermore, most hate the life they are living and would not care to celebrate, in terms of rituals, for example, anything about that life. Thus these homeless people appear not to share a subculture, which is why, despite their apparent tie to a place, they are best viewed as not composing an enclave.[6]

ENCLAVE BOUNDARIES

Some enclaves have intentionally designed entries that unambiguously mark some or all of their boundaries. In San Francisco, for example, portals over main streets leading into Chinatown have elaborate decorations to mark them as entrances. Some neighborhoods in Chicago have erected signs on major thoroughfares leading into particular areas (such as "Welcome to Rogers Park") or put neighborhood name signs on light poles at major intersections. More often there is no intentional designation of an entrance or a boundary, and people have only mental images of where socially significant places are located.

Around 1920, Ernest Burgess, who spent many years collaborating with Robert Park, prepared a "Fact Book" for Chicago. This book identified seventy-five communities, almost all of which were informal rather than formal entities; their names did not appear on city maps and they did not correspond with legal jurisdictions. Most consisted of residential areas surrounding a local shopping area, park, or school that residents regarded as the center of the community. About fifty years later, Albert Hunter, a graduate student in sociology at the University of Chicago, found that some of the communities Burgess noted had simply disappeared, others had changed names, and still others had merged into larger areas.[7] However, nearly one-half persisted intact, suggesting to Hunter that community names are part of a shared local culture and, therefore, endure. He also asked his respondents to identify, if they could, the boundaries of the community in which they lived. About 70 percent could name four boundaries, typically being boulevards, expressways, parks, and so on.

Regardless of their obtrusiveness, boundary markers are rarely associated with abrupt and total changes in community composition. Places usually change from each other in subtle ways that become dramatic only after they have accumulated. Residents' dress, their skin color, the music they are playing, and the food in store windows all provide clues to the changes that are occurring in the composition of an area. The distinctive features of an enclave, in most instances, gradually crystallize as one moves from its periphery to its core. For example, the Greenpoint section of Brooklyn contains a white, European (largely Polish) residential and commercial area. Packed into several blocks are Polish restaurants and meat markets, busts of Polish heroes, and billboards written in Polish. Adjacent to this enclave is a section with a Hispanic concentration, many of whose residents work in local factories. A resident described how one could see the racial differences between the geographical center of Greenpoint and its boundaries: "You go to Greenpoint Avenue and down . . . you'll see . . . white and Hispanic. But if you go all the way up . . . they're all white."[8]

It should also be recognized that distinctions made by local residents are likely to be more precise than those made by people farther away. Outsiders may simply be unaware of boundaries that separate enclaves (or subenclaves) from each other within an area. For instance, during the late 1950s Herbert Gans studied an inner-city Boston area called "West End." The single largest group in the area consisted of first- and second-generation Italian households. Other large immigrant groups were Polish, Jewish, and Irish. There was also a "skid row" area populated mostly by single men who drifted and drank.

internal distinction

To the average person who resided elsewhere in Boston, Gans wrote, the West End was one undifferentiated slum. However, "the concept of the West End as a single neighborhood was foreign to the West Enders themselves."[9]

Corresponding with the tendency for different West Enders to see themselves as residing in separate enclaves were the specialized stores and institutions of each group. The Jewish area of the West End, although holding only about 10 percent of the total West End population, maintained two synagogues with a full range of social and religious activities, a Hebrew school, Jewish restaurants, and kosher food stores. Despite some intermingling of Jewish and Italian commercial and residential sites, especially near the enclaves' shared borders, the Jewish residents thus appeared to have formed a separate enclave.

The difference between the self-views of people who lived in the West End and the views of non–West Enders existed because the latter tended to avoid the area. They knew too little about it to make many distinctions. In addition, to non–West Enders, many of the differences emphasized by the people of the West End would likely have been of trivial importance. The residents were recent immigrants, they were generally poor, and they lived in a run-down neighborhood. For purposes of social placement, that was probably all the other Bostonians cared to know.

class

The difficulty of identifying boundaries makes it impractical to study enclaves using any of the large-scale databases that have been compiled. Census Bureau publications, zip code directories, and other publications contain voluminous information about communities and neighborhoods, but they do not indicate where enclaves exist between and among neighborhoods and communities. To locate enclaves with any precision requires detailed, first-hand information about a place that can be obtained only by walking its streets.[10]

method

IDENTITY AND PLACE

We have referred to enclaves as areas containing residents who share something significant. This expression is intended to convey not only that residents are alike in some regard, but that the residents themselves are aware of the commonality and that the shared quality is important to their identities. From a social-psychological perspective, the term *identities* refers to people's definitions of their (social) selves and tends to be linked to roles and statuses. Most people occupy numerous roles, are involved in many different relationships, and have multiple identities. Thus, when they think about who they are, people view themselves in occupational or student roles, familial roles, gender and racial roles, and the like.

role status

Some roles are highly situational, and the identities associated with them also tend to vary situationally. Suppose a person were either markedly older or younger than everyone else in a particular group. While in that group, in contrast with a mixed-age group, that person would likely see age as a more salient aspect of his or her identity.

Some statuses are less prone to situational change. They remain central features of a person's identity. One useful way to distinguish among the many specific roles or statuses in a person's repertoire is in terms of the "identity salience" of each.[11] The roles that people bring to many different situations are likely to have high identity salience. For example, if a hypothetical physician, "Dr. Smith," insisted on being described as *Dr.* Smith in voter registration files, on being introduced as *Dr.* Smith in social settings, and made restaurant and hotel reservations as *Dr.* Smith, it would probably indicate that the doctor role had a high identity salience for that physician. Enclave names, simultaneously conveying both physical and social space, can similarly attain very high salience in people's identities.[12] The names of communities of this type serve as anchors for residents' identities. Saying that one is from the Castro district or Kiryas Joel or the West End is a personal statement that acts as a calling card, providing others inside and outside of the enclave with information about the person's status and identity.

Another way to differentiate among roles or statuses in terms of their salience for people's identities is to note the emotional difficulty that people ordinarily experience when they go through the process of disengaging from them. The role exits that usually create the greatest turmoil for people—sex changes, giving up custody of children, or leaving a profession—are the ones associated with people's most salient identities.[13] Disruptions in the roles associated with people's place attachments, due to natural disasters, for example, have similarly been found to have profoundly adverse effects on people. The more enclave qualities that communities have before a flood, landslide, or the like, the greater the long-term depression, sadness, and stress former residents report feeling after they are forced to move. Some go through a grieving process for the destroyed place similar to a mourning for the dead.[14]

There can also be emotional aftereffects when urban renewal projects or racial and economic changes in communities pressure people to leave enclaves. For example, a few dozen Jewish men originally from the Brownsville section of eastern Brooklyn hold an annual reunion in New York's Catskills in order to reminisce about their old neighborhood. When they were growing up in the 1940s, Brownsville was a Jewish enclave. It began to change in the 1960s, and everyone the men knew from the old days has moved or died. The synagogues and the shops are also gone. The place that was their enclave is no more, but now they come from across the country to meet every year because the Brownsville of their youth is still an important part of their identities. However, the only sense in which they can still go home (and resume former roles) is by reliving together the significant events of their collective past.[15]

DOMINANT STATUSES

There appear to be many instances in which "outsiders" attempt to more or less equate people with a single master status. For example, to whites, blacks may be only blacks—it does not matter whether they are fat or thin, smart or dumb. Of course, blacks may also disregard similar differences among whites. In the same way, straight people may equate gay people with a sexual orientation, and vice versa. The one status that is dominant, or overwhelming, in the eyes of others can also be based on a person's occupation (e.g., movie star), past history (e.g., ex-con), or physical condition (e.g., blind).

Because others tend to recognize only the one status, it is important for people with a potentially dominant status who are committed to multiple statuses to interact with others like themselves. Such others are often the only ones who can "validate" the full range of a person's salient identities. If a woman is to continue to view herself as humorous, for example, it is necessary for people to laugh when she tells stories; if a man is to continue to think of himself as physically attractive, it is necessary for others to respond to him in an interested way. When people with a potentially dominant status—such as openly gay, black, or Chinese—interact with others who do not share that status, the others may be overwhelmed by that one master status. As a result, the outsiders may not respond to the person's humor, physical attributes, and so on. That leaves the person with only the single identity when interacting with others who are different. Thus people with such dominant statuses typically prefer each other's company.[16] The homogeneity of enclaves with respect to the dominant status translates into opportunities for people to establish their other identities and provides one explanation for why many people are reluctant to leave enclaves.

With respect to enclave formation, people with two or more potentially dominant statuses present an especially interesting case. One strategy such persons have followed is to play the roles associated with the different statuses sequentially, and to play the roles with different others (i.e., keep audiences segregated). This tactic may minimize the role conflicts a person experiences, but it does not eliminate all the stress that person may feel. To illustrate, an African American lesbian explained that there is always a debate in her mind over whether to emphasize being black or gay, but added, "You can't stop being one. We've done that too long. Saying, 'I'm going to be black when I go to the N.A.A.C.P.

meeting, so I'll stop being gay right now.' Or, 'I'm going to sit in on the Gay Pride community meeting, so I'm going to stop being black.'"[17]

At the same time, conflicts periodically arise between groups to which people are simultaneously tied, and those people may be forced to choose sides, that is, decide which of their identities takes precedence. In San Francisco in 1993, for example, an African American preacher presented to his congregation what he termed a literal interpretation of the Bible. To many who heard the talk he appeared to be condoning violence against homosexuals. As a result of the ensuing controversy, the city mayor dismissed the pastor from the San Francisco Human Rights Commission. African American civic leaders then lined up behind the pastor, thereby aligning themselves against the gay community. Gay African Americans were caught in the middle, which led to the eventual creation of new organizations that attempted to again fuse African American and gay identities.[18]

In large cities people are less likely to be forced to choose among dominant identities, because of the possibility of forming organizations that combine multiple statuses. In New York, for example, there are all-white gay clubs, all-black gay clubs, all-Latino gay clubs. These combinations of dominant statuses can also be a factor in encouraging people to establish subenclaves. Thus a gay subenclave may form within a larger enclave in which the residents are predominantly African American or young professionals, for instance. Or within a predominantly gay enclave, there may be subenclaves that differ from each other in terms of such aspects as social class or race. The places where these multiple-status subenclaves form are often "social borderlands"—fringe areas in which, by straddling different groups, people create new social forms in terms of language, dress, style, or the like.[19]

THE FORMATION OF ENCLAVES

Enclaves typically grow by serving as magnets that attract other people who share the same significant quality as the pioneers. For a place to seem as though it is dominated by a particular group, and to then act like a magnet to others, the group need not make up 100 percent, or even a majority, of the local population. If no other group is present in sizeable numbers and the distinctive group's institutions and stores are concentrated in conspicuous locations, then an area could appear to be dominated by a group that comprised 25 percent or less of its population.[20]

An interesting and logically prior question concerns why enclaves form where they do. Closeness to places of work associated with members of the distinctive group is often one reason the "settlers" chose a particular

residential area. During the early part of the nineteenth century, for exam-
ple, the first of many Norwegian immigrants settled in Brooklyn, New
York, near the East River. They selected this part of Brookyln because of its
proximity to the docks and harbors, where they were initially employed.
Similarly, a young and politically active gay enclave formed in West
Hollywood, California, apparently because of its closeness to the film,
recording, television, and design industries in Hollywood, where many of
West Hollywood's residents were employed.[21] In addition, the pioneers of
enclaves sometimes select a particular site because of its physical features.
For example, the Norwegians were attracted to the area near the Brooklyn
shipyards because the salt water and ships made them feel "at home."[22]

Sometimes a specific place seems to be selected simply because it is
available when a distinctive group needs a place, and no one else wants it.
For example, right after the notorious stock market crash of 1929, a large
reservoir in New York's Central Park was drained and taken out of service.
A few homeless people immediately set up residence in the reservoir but
were evicted by the police. Over the next two years, as the Great Depression
worsened, more homeless people moved to the park and built small shacks.
Evictions and arrests for vagrancy slowly declined and the shantytown's
population grew into the hundreds. Most of the shacks had chairs and
beds, some had carpets, and the shack of some unemployed bricklayers
even had an inlaid tile roof. The shantytown became known as "Hoover
Valley," and its unpaved road as "Depression Street." City officials became
concerned with sanitation in the settlements and the possibility that the
homeless men were really just disorderly vagrants. In 1933 the city resumed
work on the reservoir landfill, and Hoover Valley was dismantled.[23]

The prior settlement of a place by people with similar characteristics
has always been a major magnet to later migrants. The movers who follow
later know of the enclave's existence before they relocate, and it becomes
their intended destination. The pioneers who become established in the
enclave often intentionally recruit potential migrants, and they typically
provide many types of help to newcomers, such as monetary assistance,
employment, or help in finding an apartment.

Attraction to an enclave can also be based on the goods and services
that are exclusively offered in its specialized stores and institutions. It is usually only in enclaves that there are the concentrated numbers of potential
customers or clients necessary to support the purveyors of various types of
specialized goods and services. Access to them may serve as a magnet to
members of the distinctive group. In Houston, for example, there is a substantial enclave of Iranian exiles. For those who wish to follow traditional
Muslim practices in arranging and negotiating marriages, observing communal religious rites, and the like, life outside of the enclave would be

impossible. To illustrate, consider how a death in the family is to be handled. The proper traditional response includes assembling mourners in a mosque for a prayer service to ensure the deceased's passage to the next world, ritual washing of the corpse, burial in an exclusively Muslim graveyard, digging the grave exactly to the prescribed depth, and making certain the deceased faces Mecca, among other such tasks. Within the enclave it is difficult enough to find the technical skills and communal cooperation that are needed for such tasks; outside the enclave, it would probably be next to impossible.[24]

ENCLAVES AND WORLD SYSTEMS

Once enclaves are established, their subsequent growth is often the result of large-scale events that occur outside of their boundaries; for example, Hoover Valley would doubtless never have grown so large had the Great Depression not occurred. Another example is provided by the dislocation associated with World War II. The war facilitated the movement of many gay and lesbian servicepeople, after their discharge, to openly gay and lesbian enclaves in San Francisco, Los Angeles, and other coastal cities, because once they had left their small hometowns (where they had hidden their homosexuality), they did not want to return. Thus changes in the cultural, social, or economic life of a society are soon reflected in the nature and location of new residential enclaves.

Furthermore, because of the interdependence among cities and nations of the world, events that occur almost anywhere can affect distant enclaves. Thus potato famines in Ireland pushed many people to emigrate to America and settle in Irish enclaves in Boston and New York. Another example is the increase in imported goods manufactured in Southeast Asia, which hastened the conversion of former factories to loft apartments, promoting inner-city "yuppie" enclaves in Chicago, Philadelphia, and elsewhere. The specific cities in which immigrant enclaves form also illustrate patterns of international interdependence. The overwhelming majority of immigrants who came to the United States 100 years ago settled in New York City, at least initially. It was the preeminent U.S. city of the time; it housed the headquarters of major corporations and the nation's financial center and served as the country's locus of transportation and communication—it was the nation's major link to the rest of the world. Until the middle of the twentieth century, almost all of the United States's international flights arrived in and departed from New York, and the international publishing and financial institutions that were located in the United States were almost exclusively headquartered in New York.

The world economy has grown in the past fifty years or so, with the economy of each nation increasingly influenced by events occurring outside of its borders. Decisions that greatly affect millions of people are now routinely made in "global cities." These are the cities—such as London, Paris, and Tokyo—in which almost all of the world's economic activity is integrated and coordinated. The awesome efficiency of modern transportation and communication has made it possible for executives in the headquarters of a multinational corporation to control its production, sales, and marketing activities all around the world. The headquarters may be in London, production facilities may be in Taiwan, advertising may be centered in Atlanta, and the primary sales market may be Mexico City.

As ties between the United States and other nations have strengthened, the number of U.S. cities serving as important links to the world system has increased. In addition to New York, Los Angeles has become an important link to the Pacific Rim nations, Miami to the nations of South America, and so on.[25] Corresponding with the growth of global cities in the United States, the routes of immigrants to the United States have become more varied. New York City today is but one of many possible destinations. Other global cities such as Los Angeles, Miami, Chicago, and San Francisco are also major recipients of immigration. The countries of origin of the more recent immigrants also differ from their counterparts of 100 years ago. Most of the earlier arrivals were European, and the current immigrants are predominantly Hispanic (from Mexico, Cuba, etc.) and Asian (from China, Korea, etc.).[26] Despite these changes in origins and destinations, however, many patterns remain largely the same, as many of the recent immigrants continue to re-create their former ways of life in enclaves in America.

IMPOSED SEPARATION

In the preceding pages we have noted many of the ways in which enclaves form and persist by attracting residents. However, enclaves are only partially maintained by the inducements they offer or by the desires of residents to remain in homogeneous concentrations. Segregation also results from the desires of people outside of the enclave to preserve their own neighborhoods by keeping out the residents of enclaves. The boundaries of residential areas are, of course, sometimes maintained by violence. When outsiders' encroachments are defined as trespasses and physically punished, it sends a clear message to all outsiders to remain "in their place."

The boundaries of enclaves are most often maintained in more subtle ways, though. In the Greenpoint section of Brooklyn, for example, white ethnic and Hispanic enclaves sit side by side. People of European descent with apartments for rent take care to find tenants who are racially like themselves, even though such discrimination is against the law. The women in Greenpoint have taken the place of local realtors, informing family and friends when housing becomes available within their enclave. Information spreads in the women's network, in butcher shops and churches. People attached to the network then sponsor their friends or family members, and outsiders are excluded. The experience of one unsponsored couple—she is Irish and he is Puerto Rican—is illustrative. When they somehow learned of a vacant apartment in the white ethnic enclave, they were still unable to rent it. They were asked by a prospective landlord, "What are you?" She said Irish, he said Hispanic. "What kind?" the landlord asked him. When he said Puerto Rican, the landlord asked if they had "any crawling things" in their current apartment, and then refused to rent to them.[27]

People in enclaves are also kept in their places by the actions of others that set them apart. Filipinos in Salinas, California, for example, tended to remain in the Filipino enclave for fear of being rejected by Anglos. They were self-conscious about their ability to speak English, and in the work settings where they had regular contacts with Anglos, they felt ridiculed by the way Anglos spoke to them: slowly and often using incorrect grammar such as, "Work . . . difficult . . . here?"[28] In suburban Atlanta, to illustrate further, the Cobb County Board of Commissioners passed a resolution condemning homosexuality, and eliminated all fiscal year 1994 funding for the arts for fear that some of it would support "life styles advocated by the gay community."[29] To understand the context, one must know that in the summer of 1993, many people in Cobb County (and the nation) were concerned with homosexual issues such as ending their exclusion from the military and improving their treatment in school curricula. In Atlanta, at the same time, with leadership from the local gay community, the city granted domestic partnership status to the partners of gay city employees. The county commissioners then felt it was important to make a statement telling homosexuals that their life-style would not be tolerated in Cobb County.

The most effective large-scale means of keeping people in their place is probably through the official actions of cities, counties, and other municipalities. Such actions take the forms of zoning ordinances, fire and safety regulations, highway construction projects, and so on. Local governments can play an active role in maintaining the segregation of enclaves by imposing either symbolic or ecological constraints on people's movement. The former are often indirect ways of putting out an "unwelcome mat" to some groups. For example, the selective enforcement of vagrancy laws is a time-honored way of discouraging minorities or the homeless from settling in a new area, even temporarily. In many cities the location of expressways similarly reinforces enclave boundaries in a very direct manner. In Los Angeles during the 1950s, for example, a number of freeways were constructed that bounded (on all four sides) a Chicano community in East Los Angeles. The freeways effectively isolated the enclave, but its generally poor and unorganized residents were virtually powerless to stop the construction.[30]

SUMMARY AND PREVIEW

This introductory chapter has presented an overview of the theoretical issues that will constitute the core of this book. Most significant is the view that enclaves contain the following:

Concentrations of residents who share a distinctive status that is important to their identity

Specialized stores and institutions that provide local support for the residents' distinctive life-style

A strong tie between that life-style and the geographic space the residents occupy.

The place then becomes a calling card, symbolizing the social identities of the residents of the enclave.

Enclaves often act like magnets, attracting immigrants, exiles, or other migrants once an initial settlement forms. Newcomers are attracted to enclaves both for material assistance and because they are the best (or only) places in which people feel they can fully be themselves. The relative isolation of enclaves is maintained by both the wishes of residents to live apart and the animosities of outsiders, which are expressed in threats and symbols designed to keep people in their place. The actions of local governments are also very effective means of maintaining segregation.

We have proposed that the tendency to confine the term *enclave* to racial or ethnic concentrations is too limiting. Life-style and income can also be the bases of enclaves; so too can combinations of race, religion, life-style, ethnicity, and wealth. In the following chapters we will examine in detail a number of enclaves that represent a diverse array of historical and contemporary types. Each chapter presents a case study of one or two enclaves that are representative of a larger category, and in at least some respects are exemplars of that type of enclave.

The three chapters following this one are historically grounded, focusing on various types of enclaves that once were common but are rarely found in contemporary metropolitan areas. All were shaped by major features of nineteenth-century cities that subsequently changed, leading to dissolution of the distinctive enclaves within them. The final four chapters are more contemporary in their focus, as well as more regionally inclusive. The first two of these chapters examine racial–ethnic enclaves, focusing on Chinese and Cuban concentrations. They represent specific examples of the largest immigrant groups in the last third of the twentieth century: Asian and Hispanic. Both chapters examine the important differences between the enclaves of traditional immigrants and those of more recent political exiles. The final two chapters complete our survey, examining enclaves that are based on shared values and life-styles. More detailed descriptions of each chapter follow.

Chapter Two describes elite enclaves based on residents' wealth and life-style. These enclaves, typically small in size, usually involved a number of extended families connected to each other by kinship ties. Boston's Beacon Hill is the primary focus of the chapter, with secondary attention directed to Philadelphia's Chestnut Hill and San Francisco's Nob Hill. These were the exemplars of elite enclaves that developed in eastern cities early in the nineteenth century and later that century in the Midwest and West.

Chapter Three is an examination of the "Back of the Yards" area on Chicago's southwest side. This sprawling community was primarily composed of European immigrants working in the stockyards' meat-packing plants. The Yards complex illustrates the close association between neighborhood and work that was characteristic of many large American cities during the period of rapid industrial development in the late nineteenth and early twentieth centuries.

Chapter Four examines two concentrations of African Americans in the Detroit area near the turn of the twentieth century: a large and predominantly poor enclave on the near east side and a smaller and wealthier near-enclave that formed on what was then the edge of the city. During this period Detroit provides an excellent example of an industrializing city growing rapidly, because its opportunities for factory employment attracted both African American and white migrants from the South, as well as international immigrants.

Chapter Five analyzes two groups of Chinese immigrants who settled in California. In the nineteenth century the first group came penniless to prospect for gold and silver, and they established the Chinese Quarter in San Francisco, the predecessor to the city's contemporary Chinatown. In contrast, many of more recent Chinese immigrants left professional and managerial professions to flee the communists, and many of them have settled in upper-income suburban areas east of Los Angeles.

Chapter Six provides a description of several diverse waves of Cuban immigrants and exiles, most of whom have settled in the Miami area. That city's Little Havana, the primary focus of the chapter, contains the largest concentration of Cubans anywhere in the world outside of Havana.

Cohesion is maintained within the community by opposition to Castro's regime and by the persistence of distinctively Cuban ways of life, but on both of these issues there are marked generational differences.

Chapter Seven examines the largest, and commercially and institutionally the most complete, gay enclave in the United States: the Castro district in San Francisco. As an openly gay place, it is now about twenty-five years old. Like similar communities elsewhere in the United States, the Castro was a declining manufacturing area until it was revived by a gay influx. This chapter also describes the adjacent Mission district, where lesbian residents make up a near-enclave attached to the Castro district.

Chapter Eight describes Hasidic Jewish communities that settled in Brooklyn, New York, after World War II. The chapter examines the Lubavitch sect in Crown Heights, in particular. This Hasidic enclave is illustrative of many closed religious communities that have formed in the United States since its founding, but it is also unique in that the Hasidim reside in close proximity to African American and Hispanic populations. This proximity has resulted in frequent intergroup conflicts.

Chapter Nine argues that contemporary enclaves will probably be more persistent than their predecessors because the recent trend toward multiculturalism puts less emphasis on assimilation and because residents of contemporary enclaves have more wealth and power, and thus social mobility does not require movement out of the enclave. Finally, we shall examine how multiculturalism encourages distinctive local commercial activities within enclaves and how this development runs counter to the growth of franchises with standardized products that has occurred in most of the nation.

NOTES

1. Robert E. Park, "The City," in Robert E. Park, Ernest W. Burgess, and Roderick D. McKenzie (Eds.), *The City,* Chicago: University of Chicago Press, 1967, p. 40 (originally published in 1925). Park's first career was as a newspaper reporter, but when he found himself more interested in the impact of newspapers on city life than in the stories he was covering, he became an academic sociologist. See Robert E. Faris, *Chicago Sociology,* San Francisco: Chandler, 1967.

2. See, for example, Kenneth L. Wilson and W. Allen Martin, "Ethnic Enclaves," *American Journal of Sociology* 88, 1982.

3. Stephen O. Murray, "Components of Gay Community in San Francisco," in Gilbert Herdt (Ed.), *Gay Culture in America,* Boston: Beacon Press, 1992.

4. Jerome R. Mintz, *Hasidic People,* Cambridge, MA: Harvard University Press, 1992.

5. The Gypsies' prohibition on economic dealings with each other also inhibits the development of local community businesses. See Ian F. Hancock, "Gypsies," in Stephen Thernstrom (Ed.), *Harvard Encyclopedia of American Ethnic Groups,* Cambridge, MA: Harvard University Press, 1980; and Chapter Three in William M. Kephart and William W. Zellner, *Extraordinary Groups,* New York: St. Martin's Press, 1994.

6. David A. Snow and Leon Anderson, *Down on Their Luck,* Berkeley: University of California Press, 1993.

7. Albert Hunter, *Symbolic Communities,* Chicago: University of Chicago Press, 1974.

8. Judith N. DeSena, *Protecting One's Turf,* Lanham, MD: University Press of America, 1990. For further discussion of Greenpoint, see *The New York Times,* January 6, 1995, p. C1.

9. Herbert Gans, *The Urban Villagers,* New York: Free Press, 1982, p. 11.

10. One promising approach is to begin with the census tracts compiled by the Census Bureau, and then use direct observation within or between tracts to identify subareas with the qualities in question. An excellent example is provided by Paul A. Jargowsky and Mary Jo Bane, "Ghetto Poverty in the United States," in Christopher Jencks and Paul E. Peterson (Eds.), *The Urban Underclass,* Washington, DC: Brookings Institution, 1991.

11. Sheldon Stryker, *Symbolic Interactionism,* Menlo Park, CA: Benjamin Cummings, 1980.

12. Hunter, op. cit. See also David M. Hummon, "Community Attachment," in Irwin Altman and Setha M. Low (Eds.), *Place Attachment,* New York: Plenum, 1992.

13. Helen R. F. Ebaugh, *Becoming an Ex,* Chicago: University of Chicago Press, 1988, p. 171.

14. Barbara B. Brown and Douglas D. Perkins, "Disruptions in Place Attachment," in Altman and Low, op. cit.

15. Gerald Sorin, *The Nurturing Neighborhood,* New York: New York University Press, 1990.

16. Similar processes are described in Erving Goffman, *Stigma,* Englewood Cliffs, NJ: Prentice-Hall, 1963; and Ebaugh, op. cit.

17. *The New York Times,* June 28, 1993, p. A12.

18. For further discussion, see *The New York Times,* February 20, 1995, p. A13.

19. David Wellman, "Honorary Homey's, Class Brothers, and White Negroes." Paper presented at the American Sociological Association meetings, August 1993.

20. For further discussion of this issue, see Howard P. Chudacoff, *Evolution of American Urban Society,* Englewood Cliffs, NJ: Prentice-Hall, 1994.

21. E. Michael Gorman, "The Pursuit of the Wish," in Gilbert Herdt (Ed.), *Gay Culture in America,* Boston: Beacon Press, 1992.
22. Christen T. Jonassen, "Cultural Variables in the Ecology of an Ethnic Group," *American Sociological Review* 14, 1949. Similarly, many Korean and Russian immigrants have recently established small suburban enclaves in the Catskills of New York because its woods and hills remind them of their homelands. *The New York Times,* July 12, 1993, p. B5.
23. Roy Rozenzweig and Elizabeth Blackmar, *The Park and the People: A History of Central Park,* Ithaca, NY: Cornell University Press, 1992.
24. For further discussion of the (often humorous) difficulties faced by Iranians in Houston and elsewhere, see Michael M. J. Fischer and Mehdi Abedi, *Debating Muslims,* Madison: University of Wisconsin Press, 1990.
25. Saskia Sassen, *The Global City,* Princeton, NJ: Princeton University Press, 1991 and *Cities in a World Economy,* Thousand Oaks, CA: Pine Forge Press, 1994.
26. For an overview of immigration patterns, see Rita J. Simon and Susan H. Alexander, *The Ambivalent Welcome,* New York: Praeger, 1993.
27. DeSena, op. cit., p. 61.
28. Edwin B. Almirol, *Ethnic Identity and Social Negotiation,* New York: AMS Press, 1985, p. 121.
29. *The New York Times,* August 29, 1993, p. 18.
30. See Rudolfo F. Acuna, *A Community Under Siege,* Chicano Studies Research Center Publication #11, Los Angeles: The Center, University of California at Los Angeles, 1984.

2

Boston's Beacon Hill and Other Elite Enclaves

Many cities initially formed in sites that offered favorable access to rivers, lakes, or oceans because of the importance of water routes for transportation. One downside of proximity to water, however, is that flooding can be a recurring problem. The modern technology of the Army Corps of Engineers has alleviated some of the problems but not eliminated them entirely. In earlier times, 150 to 200 years ago, the risks to life and property were even more substantial. Thus the most desirable places within cities where flooding was a threat were up high, on hills. Another aspect of bodies of water is that they seem generally to hold an attraction for people. People like residences from which they can look out over rivers, lakes, and oceans, and in addition to the safety from flooding it provides, higher ground translates into better views.

It is the wealthier and more privileged classes who almost always win in the competition for the most desirable residential areas. As a result, in many cities there is a marked correlation between the social status of communities and the number of feet at which they rest above sea level. It is therefore not surprising that elite nineteenth-century communities formed in places such as Nob Hill in San Francisco, Beacon Hill in Boston, and Chestnut Hill in Philadelphia.

By the beginning of the nineteenth century, large Eastern cities had growing numbers of families that had acquired great wealth and passed it on for a sufficiently long time that their family names became synonymous with high social standing: Adams and Cabot in Boston, Biddle and Ingersoll in Philadelphia, Roosevelt and Jay in New York. The sources of these families' wealth were varied. Some had brought their money with them from England; others had acquired it in conjunction with British appointments in the colonies as governors, judges, or the like; and some had earned it in America in manufacturing, trade, or banking. What these families had in common was a distinctive social status associated with their old wealth.

ELITE STATUS GROUPS

The most important feature of *status* as we employ the term here was captured by Max Weber's distinction between status and class. By *class,* Weber meant the economic situation of people. He talked about class as comprising a person's life chances, which were determined by that person's position in the marketplace. One's *ability* to buy an elegant summer home, hire maids and cooks, and throw lavish parties, for example, would obviously require substantial wealth and therefore be a function of one's class position. By contrast, *status* for Weber was primarily defined by one's *style* of life, with its attendant degree of prestige. He recognized at least a partial economic, or class, basis for status positions; some life-styles are very expensive to maintain and hence require substantial wealth. However, he insisted on maintaining a distinction between class and status such that one would not be reduced to the other. An aspect of status, separate from class, would be involved in where one wanted a summer home, whether one entertained at home, and the kinds of entertaining one did. Weber observed that nothing could be more foreign to those of high status than the vulgar pretentiousness of people who had recently acquired great wealth and were busy spending it but had not yet learned how to consume with "taste."[1]

Nelson W. Aldrich, Jr., in reflecting on his experiences in the upper class, makes Weber's point clear when he states that the critical characteristic of the money of the "real" upper class is its longevity. In this respect money is like fine wine or cheese; it is better when aged. What is most important, of course, is not solely the age of the money, but the way its age tends to be related to the outlooks of its possessors. "Old Money," he writes, is seen by its holders as an estate, with a history that is held in trust. The income it produces is used to support a family and its cultural undertakings. Old wealth is something one simply takes for granted and passes on, and its uses are determined by traditional standards. The earners of "New Money," in contrast, see wealth as a tool with infinite possibilities and take none of its characteristics for granted. The stance is entrepreneurial, pushing aside traditional standards and seeking more and bigger marketplaces where everything is, presumably, for sale.[2]

Weber also argued that shared status was an important basis for interaction among people. In other words, he viewed people as being attracted to others on the basis not solely, or even primarily, of similar purchasing power but of shared tastes in consumption. Associations were likely to form on the basis of common status or life-style characteristics such as taste in music, clothing, or vacation sites. It is common, Weber continued, for those of any status or life-style to restrict access to their group, thereby keeping people who are deemed to be "different" outside of their social circle.

Aldrich again provides an interesting example in describing a typical Old Money social club, in which the unattractive and vulgar ways of the business class ("New Money") are eschewed. Shoptalk is prohibited at the lunch tables. Conviviality and serenity are expected to reign supreme so people can "simply be." It is actually offensive for a man to identify his job, and even bad form to introduce oneself; others are expected just to know. The Old Money club, Aldrich states, "is a refuge from the ugly world outside, with its pleading, cajoling, sleeve-plucking, breast thumping strivers and strugglers swirling through the streets."[3]

Weber concluded that restrictions on access to a social circle lead to endogamous marriages, especially in high-status groups. It is by keeping marriages within the status group that the group is, in fact, perpetuated. Because prior attainments of families, as opposed to those of individuals, are the primary basis by which the elite in America maintained the closed boundaries of their circle, Baltzell describes the American upper class as having a "clan culture." Some of the most penetrating analyses of elite circles have been provided by Baltzell, himself both an offspring of the upper class and a sociologist. To illustrate "clan culture," Baltzell presents a letter of introduction that might have been written on behalf of a proper young Philadelphian:

> Sir, allow me to introduce Mr. Rittenhouse Palmer Penn. His grandfather on his mother's side was a colonel in the Revolution, and on his father's side he is connected with two of the most exclusive families in our city . . . and his family has always lived on Walnut street . . . I feel certain that his very desirable social connections will render him of great value.[4]

Following from their pronounced interest in their own ancestors, the nineteenth-century elite formed local historical and genealogical societies. The better the documentation of ancestry, the better could family background be erected as a barrier against potential invasion by the nouveau riche. The aristocratic families also established exclusive schools and private clubs for their own use. They later played central roles in the creation of the first museums and symphony orchestras in their cities. In every realm of life they emphasized a genteel life-style (proof of "breeding") as well as family lineage to regulate access to their clubs, schools, and neighborhoods.

Elite enclaves in this country have tended to be composed of white Anglo-Saxon Protestants (WASPs), especially from the late nineteenth century onward. Prior to that time there were some Jews in exclusive clubs in

New York, San Francisco, and elsewhere, and a few had even married into elite enclaves in Philadelphia. With increasing numbers of Eastern European Jews immigrating to American cities, however, anti-Semitism grew in the late nineteenth century, especially in Boston. Harvard University, reflecting its Boston Brahmin heritage, instituted a quota system for Jewish students; the Brahmins opposed, though unsuccessfully, the appointment of Louis Brandeis (a Jew) to the Supreme Court; and Jews were excluded from the "best" clubs and neighborhoods. While Boston's elite may have been the most actively anti-Semitic, local elites in other cities more or less followed the same pattern. In Los Angeles, for example, Jews had helped to establish several of the most select social clubs during the 1880s and 1890s, but after 1900 they were excluded from them.[5]

Persons of color were rarely included in elite communities even though large numbers of nonwhite persons sometimes lived on the edges of WASP enclaves. There was a large upper-status African American community located at the base of Beacon Hill, for example, but there was virtually no social contact between the persons who lived in the enclaves at the bottom and the top of the hill.[6] Elizabeth R. Ameisen contends that for elite WASP communities to persist, they must continuously reinforce beliefs in the superiority of their way of life, requiring that their life-style be protected against any outsiders seen as trying to "infiltrate." Thus exclusion and discrimination are necessary practices of elite enclaves "to ensure that the way of life they know will continue."[7]

There was a high rate of intramarriage among the elite, who shared the same values and life-style and whose social circles were closed to outsiders. As a result, kinship ties were widespread among them, which gave them a clanlike quality and encouraged them to form residential enclaves. They were also drawn toward the same areas for access to such institutions as the elegant Episcopal churches they built and their private clubs and schools. Around the turn of the nineteenth century, a group of wealthy Bostonians met and planned what would become the prototype of all elite residential enclaves on Beacon Hill in Boston.

BUILDING BEACON HILL

Beacon was the tallest of three hills on which Boston was initially built. On its summit, the first Puritans set beacon fires to signal the approach of enemies—hence the origin of the name Beacon Hill.

During the late 1730s, Thomas Hancock bought several acres on the south slope of the hill, abutting Boston Common, and built a two-and-one-half-story mansion with dozens of rooms, including one just for household china. The house was surrounded by a number of elegant gardens and imported trees.[8] For many years the Hancock mansion was the sole edifice on the hill. The remaining acres belonged to the town and were undeveloped.

Just before the turn of the nineteenth century, an elite group of Boston Brahmins began to develop the hill into a residential area for their clan. Working in concert, they bought up land and built stately mansions with servants' quarters and decorative gardens along tree-lined streets. Long and narrow private parks with grass, flowers, and trees also ran down the center of some of the streets, where the houses, set back from the roads on both sides, all faced the park.

The housing followed a number of different designs. Early in the nineteenth century, most were Federal red brick houses or more massive, Greek-style houses built of gleaming white granite. Later in the nineteenth century there was a revival of Queen Anne design, featuring homes that were asymmetrical (for example, no two windows were alike) and made extensive use of textured materials on their facades. Many were highly decorated, with conspicuous exterior red and yellow tiles, lavender window shutters, and the like.[9]

In the past 150 years or so, newer houses have been placed between the old ones, connecting them to each other and giving the area a more crowded look than it originally possessed. Most of the ornate gardens, huge stables, and servants' quarters have also disappeared. Nonetheless, a contemporary visitor to Beacon Hill can still see some of the early brick and cobblestone sidewalks and roads. Several of the streets have retained much of their former character, and Beacon Hill continues to house some descendants of Boston's "first families."

The power of the Brahmins to influence political decisions in Boston was clearly reflected in the way in which they developed Beacon Hill. Encountering only token opposition along the way, the Brahmins were able to establish conditions that facilitated the development. Relying on connections they had made in other Boston land speculations, they were able to obtain building permits quickly and easily. When road improvements were needed to continue Beacon Hill's development, the projects were given priority and paid for by the City of Boston. With the increase in construction, land values on the hill were rising, but property on the hill was kept undervalued on city tax rolls. Beacon Hill's location near the center of Boston made it attractive to people outside of the elite enclave who wanted to commercially develop the area, but the City of Boston enacted new zoning laws and reinterpreted old ones to protect Beacon Hill from unwanted commercial enterprises that would have detracted from its residential desirability.[10]

Downtown Boston

Charles River

Back Bay

Beacon
Hill

Commercial &
Business District

Beacon Street

Boston
Common

Old
State
House

POWER AND RESISTANCE

The power of the Brahmins to develop Beacon Hill to their liking would not have been surprising to Weber. He viewed power as the influence exerted by parties—permanent or temporary associations voluntarily formed by people in order to pursue their interests in opposition to other organized groups. According to Weber, the objectives of parties could pertain primarily to values and life-styles, to economic interests, or to a combination of the two. The most powerful parties are formed by people who, by virtue of their high status in society, possess great moral authority or who, by virtue of their position in the marketplace, possess great financial resources. Either wealth or status or a combination thereof can be translated into power once parties are formed for the purpose of exerting influence. The Brahmins who set out to develop Beacon Hill had both.

Weber recognized differences in the contexts in which power could be exercised and variations in the form it might take, but his emphasis was always on power in the face of opposition. That is, he focused on situations in which there were competing parties, each trying to influence decisions that would affect all. Thus, he defined power as the probability that a party or a person "will be in a position to carry out his own will despite resistance."[11]

PARKS FOR WHOM?

One of the ways in which the interests of the upper-class residents of Beacon Hill directly opposed those of other Bostonians involved the people's use of the Boston Commons, a large park just across Beacon Street, and the smaller, private, parks throughout the enclave on the hill. Because of the density and crowding in ethnic working-class communities, working-class residents looked to parks for unrestricted recreation. To the upper class, however, the key issue was how parks could contribute to a genteel life-style. What they had in mind were parks with manicured lawns and a quiet atmosphere, in which nurses wearing white caps and aprons could stroll with baby carriages. Almost all of the uses to which the working-class people wanted to put the parks were at odds with this upper-class conception. But even though the ethnic working class far outnumbered the elite throughout New England cities during the last quarter of the nineteenth century, control over the park system (as with the rest of city government) tended to be in the hands of upper-class Yankee natives.

The activities of the working class, who viewed parks as places where they could engage in activities not possible in or around their lodgings, were offensive to upper-class tastes. The elite considered working-class people to be dirty and unkempt people who had messy picnics in the parks, drunks who were using the park to "sleep it off," immoral adolescents who were seeking sexual orgies in dark parks at night, or roughnecks who were trampling the grass with their ball games. Park commissioners tended to comply with the elite's wishes and tried to control park uses in a variety of ways such as posting "keep off the grass" signs, enforcing vagrancy laws, and erecting lights.[12]

The demands both for more parks and for the freedom to use them fully were issues that eventually transcended particular neighborhoods and ethnic groups. Parks became objects of class conflict transcending ethnic differences among the working class, who banded together in opposition to the city's elite and the city government, which the elite controlled. The conflict was initially resolved in terms highly favorable to the upper class, namely, the creation of a two-tiered system of separate and unequal parks: elaborate floral gardens in sedate settings in the elite enclaves, little more than open dumps in the working-class enclaves.

During the early years of the twentieth century, the class conflict was redefined in the writings of social reformers who urged investments in parks and playgrounds in all neighborhoods. They specifically argued that supervised play could be used to socialize working-class children into more responsible, harder-working adults. For the upper class, who owned the factories in which these children would eventually work, the arguments of the reformers justified support for public park systems. Across the country, a movement began that would lead to the formation of a National Playground Association in 1906.[13]

ECOLOGICAL POWER

Weber's writings on power and opposition have proven to be very influential. It may also be helpful, however, particularly in talking about the power of elites, to recognize a more indirect kind of power involving an ability to arrange the conditions under which people interact. Political scientist Clarence N. Stone calls this capacity *ecological power* and notes that it can be the most efficient type of power. As Weber's notion implies, it may be very difficult or very expensive or require a continuous struggle for a party to control others. But if a party can institutionalize the advantages it seeks, Stone writes, opposition may become muted, and it may be possible to circumvent many confrontations. If minority political action groups in a city are able to get affirmative action plans written into law, for example, they can forestall arguments about hiring plans for each construction project that arises. In addition, when such rules become institutionalized, they are more difficult for other parties to challenge. Thus the difficulty or expense of maintaining any political advantage is lessened if it comes to be regarded as part of the established structure within which people must interact.[14]

By focusing on the rules that govern the terms of social interaction, parties can even avoid or minimize initial opposition to their goals. More specifically, if a group has the resources to define situations, it may be able to convince local officials to reach decisions that do not appear to be detrimental to the interests of other parties. Opposing groups will not form, and the difficulty of the struggle is minimized. For example, 100 years after Beacon Hill's founding, its wealthy residents were able to obtain property tax reductions for the "historic preservation" of their neighborhood. By convincing local government officials to support their request by passing legislation in the name of preservation, their gain was apparent. The loss of revenue to the local government, or the consequences of such a diminution, may not even have been recognized by potential antagonists. However, if the issue had been expressed in terms of a tax break rather than historic preservation, other parties would have been more likely to band together in opposition to it. Thus one very important type of power can lie in the ability simply to decide what to call something.

It is the elite—whether their positions are based on status, wealth, or a combination of the two—that are most likely to have the capacity to structure the social and physical environment in a way that suits their interests, without provoking opposition. They have wielded this ecological power locally to establish and maintain elite enclaves in several American cities.

OTHER ELITE ENCLAVES

Similar elite enclaves were begun in the early and middle 1800s in other Eastern cities, and in the late 1800s in Western cities. In Philadelphia at the turn of the nineteenth century, for example, an elite enclave was formed on Chestnut Hill. Known for its chestnut trees, this hill was the highest point between Trenton, New Jersey, and Bryn Mawr, Pennsylvania. Like Beacon Hill in Boston, Chestnut Hill did not simply form unplanned. Its major period of growth, during the late nineteenth century, was directed by Henry Howard Houston, whose wealth came from oil investments, the railroad, and other land speculation in Philadelphia. He obtained permits, got the city to build roads, commissioned architects, and oversaw the building of approximately 100 mansions. His efforts turned Chestnut Hill into what was then called "Philadelphia's prettiest suburb."[15]

This Philadelphia neighborhood, like Beacon Hill, historically has contained the highest proportion of "Social Register" families in the Philadelphia metropolitan area. Also like Beacon Hill, it has its private schools and clubs and an unwelcoming attitude toward newcomers. Baltzell described Chestnut Hill as parochial and ethnocentric, with "all the qualities of the small village: the social life is inbred . . . everyone knows everyone else; gossip travels very fast."[16]

Distinguished lineages and homes in the proper neighborhoods were strongly correlated. In combination, they constituted a virtually impenetrable barrier to those outside the social and geographic inner circle. One very wealthy young man, who was excluded from Philadelphia's elite because his father's family's money was too recently acquired, explained that his mother, who came from old money, had "married across the tracks." His father's father had been poor, and worked in a butcher shop. He (the grandfather) later became fabulously wealthy and built a fine mansion, but not in the elite enclave. Therefore, he said, it was "in Nobody's Land—socially." Despite their wealth, his grandson complained, "society called him and his sons *nouveau riche*."[17]

The growth of San Francisco's Nob Hill during the 1870s was in part a replay of the development of the elite enclaves in other sections of the country. There were differences, however, associated with the region and its later development: Mining was creating enormous fortunes overnight; more of the upper-class population of Western cities was composed of recent migrants; and improved modes of intracity transportation, such as cable cars, were facilitating movement out from the center of the city. All of these factors came together to influence the development of the legendary Nob Hill.

In 1870, Rincon Hill was probably the most fashionable residential area in San Francisco. The established old money families of Rincon Hill did not welcome as neighbors the people with newer money made from mining and land speculation. However, the cable car had made the summit of Russian Hill, to the north, accessible, and the newer-moneyed people and newer arrivals to San Francisco moved there. The Higgins mansion (Mrs. Higgins was the daughter of the Attorney General of Kentucky) was the first to be built, in 1872. It contained sixty rooms with high ceilings, marble steps, and enormous bay windows overlooking the Golden Gate. The second home was built by Mr. Higgins's brother-in-law, and then others followed, each more lavish than the last. Most employed a full housekeeping staff, including chefs, and contained splendid ballrooms and gardens in which to entertain families from neighboring estates or other comparable enclaves in the city. The tendency of these people to "hobnob" with each other led to the summit of Russian Hill becoming known as Nob Hill.[18]

PRESERVING BEACON HILL

From their initial development in the early 1800s through roughly the middle of the twentieth century, the greatest threats to the continuation of specific elite enclaves came in the form of competition from newer residential areas. Automobiles and commuter trains facilitated travel, leading to the development of fashionable new residential areas that could sometimes offer more land and hence larger homes, bigger gardens, and more privacy. And if some outsiders had managed to "infiltrate" over the years, then starting a new enclave somewhere else could seem desirable to many wealthy families. However in a number of cases, the original enclaves remained, in what is at least to some degree recognizable form. Beacon Hill again provides an interesting case study, but it is exceptional in its success in retaining Boston's elite. This success has not been fully matched by the enclaves that were its contemporaries.

In Boston in the early 1900s, a new area called Back Bay was developed. An elegant community adjacent to Beacon Hill, it came to be defined as "Boston's most fashionable," and a number of the old families left the hill. As they left, the profile of Beacon Hill changed. Mansions were converted into rooming houses and a new class of people moved in, along with a plethora of commercial shops. Property values began to fall, permitting still further invasions, pushing more families off the hill, and so on in a continuing cycle.

For over a decade, the number of Boston's Social Register families living on Beacon Hill declined, while there was a corresponding increase in Back Bay.[19]

However, Beacon Hill still had a rich, long-standing symbolic value for Boston's elite, and when they banded together, their wealth and power were substantial. They outbid the competition for available mansions, which they collectively purchased, modernizing the interiors and then selling them to individual families. Apartment-hotels and various specialty shops were then denied access to locations on the hill. Further attrition of elite families from the hill was reduced, and there was a return flow. By the 1940s, Beacon Hill's percentage of Boston's Social Register families was actually twice its pre-1900 figure.

Until the 1950s each parcel of land that became available triggered a competition between elite families, who wanted the hill to retain its status as a residential area, and the commercial interests who would have liked to exploit its proximity to the center of Boston. In the late 1950s, the Beacon Hill Association was able to get the hill designated as a historical district, and a board was established to review all restoration and renovation plans. Zoning ordinances were also passed to promote the hill's use as a distinguished residential area. Thus, using Stone's terms as introduced earlier, the ecological power of the elite provided them with the capacity to reshape the environment without a series of continuing confrontations. Their wealth, contacts, and prestige and their ability to appeal to preservationist values furnished the elite the *power to* institutionally structure arrangements rather than a *power over* any specific group.

Every formerly elite enclave, including Beacon Hill, has been transformed to some degree. Some have not managed to survive at all, and many others are barely recognizable in comparison with their earlier forms. The upper-class cores of the enclaves tend to be smaller in size, and the homogeneity of the residents has declined, in terms both of residents' characteristics and of diversity of land uses. There has also been a marked decline in the degree to which a range of social activities important to upper-class life has continued to occur within the enclave.

There are a number of reasons for these changes in elite enclaves. We have already noted one: the fact that the expansion of cities, facilitated by modern modes of transportation, resulted in greater dispersal of all segments of the population. From just a few centrally located neighborhoods, the cities' upper classes have moved to many, more dispersed, city and suburban communities, resulting in less concentrated numbers in each of those communities.

The solidarity of upper-class enclaves has also been diminished by changes in marriage and divorce patterns. As was previously discussed, upper-class culture in American cities was very clannish. High rates of marriage within the local upper class provided important bonds among people in these enclaves. Divorce was almost unheard-of; thus there were few messy divorces and remarriages to complicate relationships among people who worked together, lived together, and belonged to the same clubs.

Baltzell states that the threat of informal sanctions imposed by the family was very strong when divorce was contemplated by people in upper-class enclaves. The Episcopal Church, to which most of the urban elite belonged, was closer to Catholicism on this issue than most other Protestant denominations; it did not recognize the remarriage of divorced persons. In addition to the sanctions of family and Church, divorced persons were automatically excluded from important upper-class social functions such as Assembly Balls (which were near the apex of local social activities). As late as 1940, Baltzell reports, less than 1 percent of the persons listed in Philadelphia's Who's Who were then divorced.[20]

FROM LOCAL TO NATIONAL ELITES

During the twentieth century the scene of the action changed from local cities to the nation and the world. Corporations spanned the entire United States rather than being confined to local markets, and ownership of these giant corporations typically moved from families to institutional stockholders. Corporations began to recruit their elite more from across the nation than from among members of an owning family. Even so, the new recruits to the boardroom frequently came from the same distinguished private universities, were often members of the same private clubs, and regularly sat together on the boards of many other corporations. Thus they were similar in terms of background, life-style, and social contacts, and they formed a social network, but they were not bound to each other by kinship or by a tie to one particular place.[21]

In a contemporary study of upper-class women in a Midwestern city, sociologist Susan A. Ostrander's subjects commented on birthrights and birthplaces. The women continued, like their nineteenth-century counterparts, to emphasize the importance their circle placed on being well born or from an old-line family. However, those who were fourth- and fifth-generation members of their city's elite were also aware that they were starting to be outnumbered by people who were not natives: upper-class newcomers from other cities.[22]

Despite the partial fusing of local and national upper classes, many of the local civic concerns of the old-money elite continue to set the agenda for the class. For example, groups comprising both national and local elites from business, politics, and the arts undertake to support specific cities' museums, symphonies, and libraries. Large contributions from people of high class standing enable them to "buy" status through the association of their names with visible philanthropic or cultural activities; and the special balls and opening nights sponsored by the beneficiary institutions are important places to be seen if one wants to be considered as someone socially important. However, the elite patrons are no longer drawn exclusively from the city that houses the particular cultural entity.

To sum up, the elite enclaves that have persisted until the end of the twentieth century are typically very small. The upper class of cities now lives in more dispersed locations and contains a mixture of natives and migrants from other cities. In contemporary cities there is also more mixing of old and new money. Perhaps because nuances regarding family background are less well known to people raised in different cities, the boundaries of the upper class appear to be more penetrable than they were 100 years ago. With respect to upper-class clubs, for example, Ostrander reports that membership continues to require the same values, attitudes, and life-style, helping to ensure that the class will not dramatically change. However, the gradual absorption of "a few carefully selected 'new' persons of wealth, status, and power . . . protects the class from complete stagnation."[23]

NOTES

1. Max Weber, *The Theory of Social and Economic Organization* (Trans. by A. M. Henderson and Talcott Parsons), New York: Oxford University Press, 1947.
2. See the introduction in Nelson W. Aldrich, Jr., *Old Money*, New York: Alfred A. Knopf, 1988.
3. Aldrich, op. cit., p. 51.
4. E. Digby Baltzell, *The Philadelphia Gentlemen*, New Brunswick, NJ: Transaction Books, 1989, p. 31. (The first edition was published in 1958.) Baltzell argued that Bostonians went back more generations than Philadelphians, and that the latter were more concerned with purely economic accomplishments. However, generalization about the importance of ancestry seems to hold for the elite in all cities. See also E. Digby Baltzell, *Puritan Boston and Quaker Philadelphia*, New York: Free Press, 1979.
5. Frederic C. Jaher, *The Urban Establishment*, Urbana: University of Illinois Press, 1982.
6. There were similar concentrations of upper-status African Americans in a number of cities in the late nineteenth century, but their communities were usually not true enclaves. See, for example, the discussion of the upper-status African American near-enclave in Detroit in Chapter Four.

7. Elizabeth R. Ameisen, "Exclusivity in an Ethnic Elite," in Philip L. Kilbride, et. al (Eds.), *Encounters with American Ethnic Cultures,* Tuscaloosa: University of Alabama Press, 1990, p. 76.

8. William H. Fowler, Jr., *The Baron of Beacon Hill,* Boston: Houghton Mifflin, 1980.

9. Douglas S. Tucci, *Built in Boston,* Boston: New York Graphic Society, 1978.

10. Jaher, op. cit.

11. Weber, op. cit., p. 152.

12. See the description of class conflict over parks in Worcester, Massachusetts, in Roy Rosenzweig, *Eight Hours for What We Will,* Cambridge: Cambridge University Press, 1983.

13. The association's efforts were initially directed at improving facilities for boys only. It was not until nearly 1920, in conjunction with efforts to extend women's rights to participate in many realms, that a "play-for-all" drive was extended to include improvements in girls' recreational facilities as well. See Karla A. Henderson, "A Feminist Analysis of Selected Professional Recreational Literature About Girls/Women from 1907–1990," *Journal of Leisure Research* 25, 1993.

14. Clarence N. Stone, "Power and Social Complexity," in Robert J. Waste (Ed.), *Community Power,* Beverly Hills, CA: Sage, 1986. A similar view of power within cities is presented by John R. Logan and Harvey L. Molotch, *Urban Fortunes,* Berkeley: University of California Press, 1987.

15. Richard Webster, *Philadelphia Preserved,* Philadelphia: Temple University Press, 1976.

16. Ibid., p. 205.

17. Baltzell, *The Philadelphia Gentlemen,* op. cit., p. 165.

18. Julia C. Altrocchi, *The Spectacular San Franciscans,* New York: E. P. Dutton, 1949, p. 101.

19. Walter Firey, "Sentiment and Symbolism as Ecological Variables," *American Sociological Review* 10, 1945.

20. Baltzell, *The Philadelphia Gentlemen,* op. cit. His figure refers to those currently (i.e., 1940) divorced and not remarried, rather than the sum of all those persons who had ever been divorced; but it is clear that the latter number was also extremely low in comparison with today's figures.

21. See Donald A. Palmer and Roger Friedland, "Corporation, Class and City System," in Mark S. Mizruchi and Michael Schwartz (Eds.), *Intercorporate Relations,* Cambridge: Cambridge University Press, 1987. See also Michael Useem, *The Inner Circle,* New York: Oxford University Press, 1984.

22. Susan A. Ostrander, *Women of the Upper Class,* Philadelphia: Temple University Press, 1984.

23. Ostrander, op. cit., p. 110.

3

"Back of the Yards" Chicago and Other Working-Class Enclaves

In most American cities during the early 1800s, there was little separation between the locations of work and residence. Shoemakers made shoes in the front rooms of their homes; small groups of men rolled cigars in the local tobacco store while the proprietor's family lived upstairs. Carpet weavers and small machine shops sat among row houses and tenements. A few small manufacturing concentrations—textiles, woodworking, leather goods, meat packinghouses—were also just beginning to appear in areas immediately surrounding the financial and retail centers of the downtowns.[1]

The invention of various machines in the middle of the century gradually facilitated larger concentrations of labor. Manufacturing moved from homes to factories, and production came to rely on a larger and more complex division of labor. Because the work was mechanized, the biggest demand was for unskilled labor, and a ready supply was provided by the European immigrants who began flooding into America during the last half of the nineteenth century. The unskilled workers and their families tended to concentrate around the large factories that employed them, which resulted in working-class enclaves. Because immigrants from a given country tended to cluster in a particular industry, many of the working-class enclaves were composed largely of people from the same country of origin: Slavs clustered around steel factories in Buffalo, German meat packers and their families near the Chicago stockyards, and so on.

Chicago's rapid growth during the middle of the nineteenth century was in large part a result of the railroad and westward expansion. Almost every rail line in the nation west of Lake Michigan was linked to Chicago. By 1860, these tracks resembled the spokes of a wheel, dividing the western region into pie-shaped wedges, each of which was linked to Chicago.[2] Hogs, sheep, cows, and other livestock were increasingly shipped by rail to

33

railroad

**South Chicago
Stockyards Area (1930)**

packinghouses on the southwest side of Chicago, about five miles from the downtown. In 1865 all the packing operations were consolidated when Union Stock Yards was opened. The subsequent development of refrigerated rail cars and improvements in canning made it increasingly practical to slaughter livestock in a single location. Swift, Armour, and other major meat packers located nearby, and by 1910 the complex, which included rail lines, slaughterhouses, and packing and canning houses, covered 500 acres and had its own power station.

LIVING CONDITIONS

Residential construction followed the growth of employment in the Yards. Some homes were built by residents on land owned by meat-packing companies, a few areas were developed by Armour and other meat-packing companies specifically for employees, some private developers built subdivisions, and some residential areas just sprang up in a jumble on land adjacent to the Yards. The typical home was a small, two-story, wooden frame house that covered about 60 percent of its lot. The amount of open space this left between cottages concealed the actual degree of crowding in the neighborhood.[3]

Crowded was the word that best described living conditions in Back of the Yards at the turn of the twentieth century. Most of the Catholic immigrants who lived in the Yards had very large families, a fact which by itself would have been sufficient to create crowded conditions in the small housing units. Even so, many owners and primary tenants also took in boarders. Over one-quarter of the entire Back of the Yards population lived as boarders with other families, and that figure would be substantially higher if one looked only at adults. In 1908, Milton B. Hunt, an early social researcher, canvassed thirteen blocks in the stockyards district and found that 213 families did not have lodgers but over 400 did. Of those who did, approximately 40 percent had three or more lodgers. Each lodger's rent included meal preparation but not food. The housekeeper typically kept a separate grocery ledger for each boarder and at mealtime would serve each boarder exactly the food that had been purchased on his or her behalf.[4] One can imagine how awkward some of the meals must have been, given variations in the quality and quantity of food being eaten by people at the same table.

At night, lodgers typically slept in the same rooms as family members, often in the same beds! Some slept in a bedroom, and others slept in the kitchen, which in many homes served as an additional bedroom at night. As a result of the crowding it was very difficult for married couples to obtain any kind of privacy. Arranging for sexual relations, personal family discussions, and childbirth required delicate negotiations. One woman who was raised in the Yards remembers when her mother went into labor with a younger sibling. The boarder told her to go outside and watch the chimney: "Any minute the stork's going to fly over." She waited for about four hours, heard an infant's cries, then went back into the house confused. "Somehow you missed him," the boarder explained.[5]

For some families, taking in a boarder was probably a matter of choice—to supplement family income or temporarily accommodate a relative or friend. For many families, however, it was a matter of necessity. A paying boarder was the only way they could make monthly payments. Rents were high relative to factory wages, and landlords justified this fact by pointing to the presence of boarders who were paying the primary tenants. So the landlords raised the rents further, which led residents to seek additional boarders, which justified further rent increases, and so on.

Located near the outskirts of the Yards were some once-fashionable homes that had been converted into rooming houses. This was a common practice in American cities at the turn of the twentieth century, when growth and expansion led to the decline of many residential areas. Some reasonably large single-family homes were deserted by residents who wanted to move farther away from encroaching immigrant settlements or smelly factories. The conversion of these homes into rooming houses provided a major addition to the housing stock of the period. The rooms attracted a diverse and colorful assortment of occupants. A canvass of people living in furnished rooms in Chicago at this time disclosed a great number of single men, many of whom found occasional work in factories and were described as having drinking and/or gambling problems. The investigators also reported such room occupants as a husband and wife, both of whom were heavy drinkers, in a single room with seven children whom they regularly sent out begging; and a woman with four children who cleaned offices at night and liked living in a rooming house because her children would be around other people while she was away.[6]

Descriptions of physical conditions in the Back of the Yards area painted a dismal picture. Smoke from factories and wood stoves fouled the air and produced high rates of lung disease. Rats the size of cats ran down the poorly paved streets at night, and there were swarms of flies in the filthy alleys where the children played. The smells of rotten meat, fumes from fertilizer factories, the nearby city dump, and poor sewerage facilities pervaded the air. One company regularly left an open wagon filled with bits of meat and globs of fat sitting out in the sun every day. The stench reached across the neighborhood and sickened riders in nearby streetcars. One visitor to the area later recalled getting off one streetcar and onto another because she associated a particular passenger who boarded the first streetcar with the sickening odor. In addition to the foul air and odors, the Yards' residents had to contend with the screeching and puffing of locomotives, constant bells signaling the stops and starts of streetcars, noisy trucks, and loud whistles from the factories.[7]

Death rates from some childhood diseases were two to five times higher in the Back of the Yards than in other Chicago communities. Physical conditions contributed to this problem, as did the limited medical care received by Back of the Yards families. Physicians were never engaged short of serious emergencies, because of their cost and most families' skeptical views of the medical profession. Neighborhood midwives assisted with births, and mothers tried various home remedies with sick children. If their concoctions of soap and herbs and plants did not work, the next step was typically to consult the local pharmacist. Most drugstores contained eight to ten chairs for customers waiting for a consultation. After listening to the symptoms, the pharmacist prepared an appropriate medicine and charged only for its cost.[8]

Other explanations at the time for the Yards' high child mortality rates were interesting, if one can indulge a little levity in a matter of such gravity. For example, Charles Bushnell completed one of the first doctoral dissertations in sociology at the University of Chicago in 1901. He studied living conditions in the Back of the Yards community and seems to have been one of the first scholars to condemn the evils of junk food. In summarizing his findings, he presented various child mortality rates that he related to the general health conditions of the district, citing inadequate sewerage, the squalor and dirt of the neighborhood—and the children's nonnutritious diet. "A mere glance into the lunch boxes of school children," he wrote, "shows . . . cakes, jellies and unwholesome pastry . . . " for which the children "seem to have almost a special craving."[9]

During the 1920s and 1930s, many of the graduate students of Robert Park and other professors at the University of Chicago continued the research previously begun by Bushnell. At that time the Polish enclave in the Yards was especially large, and it was the subject of several studies on family life and adolescence. According to the researchers, these studies showed that family disorganization, delinquency, alcoholism, and other social problems were a result of the general processes of acculturation and social change that all immigrants go through, and were not caused by any intrinsic aspect of Polish culture or personality. However, community cooperation with these sociological studies eventually became problematic because many Poles resented public discussions of their drinking and delinquency, so they regarded the studies as slanderously anti-Polish.[10]

SEPARATE ETHNIC VILLAGES

Outsiders would see only class, but insiders know the difference

The residential area known as Back of the Yards had reasonably distinct geographic boundaries and its residents shared similar life-styles, but it actually comprised a number of separate enclaves at the turn of the twentieth century. Each enclave consisted of core groups of 50 to 100 persons bonded by kinship that were tied to other core groups of persons of the same nationality. Common language and culture and the same churches and church-related organizations forged core groups into what have been called "old world villages." Because the Yards contained a number of such ethnic "villages," it was not, circa 1900, a single community. It was, Slayton writes, "an industrial neighborhood dominated by one form of community structure of which there were numerous examples."[11]

The first large ethnic group to move to the Yards area was Irish, and the packinghouse area initially had a strong Irish identity. (As explained in Chapter One, for an area to have an ethnic identity it is not necessary for a majority of its residents to be of that background. A relatively small percentage can appear to dominate if the group's institutions and stores are conspicuously placed and no other sizeable group is present.) The Irish influence was evident when a large meat-packing warehouse was christened "Castle Garden," after the name of New York's port of entry, because

Irish immigrants were said to go immediately to the Yards in Chicago after docking in New York. They established a parish, Saint Rose of Lima, which along with its school was a focal institution for the immigrants. By 1900 Saint Rose's membership had risen to 700 Irish families, and the area in which the Irish predominated was known as Roseville. During the same period, a large number of German families moved into another Back of the Yards area, one developed by a German entrepreneur. They also established distinctive communities with their own churches and schools, but in each area there was some intermingling and overlap of groups. The next large groups to move into the Yards were Polish, Lithuanian, and Italian.

Each nationality group established its own parish churches and schools, as well as its own distinctive restaurants and retail shops. For example, in the Polish area near the Stockyards, saloons with Polish bartenders and clienteles proliferated. If a German or other "outsider" came in, a fistfight was likely to occur. Around 1910, a survey disclosed an average of three saloons per block in the Polish sections of the Yards. They served as social centers, as informal employment bureaus where people found out about job opportunities, and as "banks" that would cash checks for the immigrant Poles.[12]

The recreated villages of each ethnic group were also served by separate neighborhood food stores. By the 1920s there were over 500 corner grocery stores serving the 75,000 people living in the Yards area, each operated by a shopkeeper of the same nationality as the local residents who shopped in the store. Store owners knew almost all of their customers by name, and relations were very personal. They gave pieces of candy to customers' children, bones to shoppers who planned to make soup that day, and waste products from the back of the store to customers they knew had pets. If a religious holiday or cultural celebration was coming, store owners of the same ethnicity could be counted on to provide the special items such as hams, sausages, or candles that their customers would need.[13]

MOVIES AND DANCES

By current standards, recreational opportunities were limited in Back of the Yards. Social–athletic clubs organized baseball and other sports on local streets and fields. Diverse social and religious activities were conducted in churches. There were also a number of neighborhood theaters; in fact, four movie theaters were competing with each other in the Yards by 1910. Some of the local theaters were actually grand emporiums, with padded chairs, smoking rooms, and spittoons. Each tried to attract customers by offering complete shows, which often included a double feature; a vaudeville show, usually featuring comedians; and for the kids, on Saturdays, a serial—an adventure series shown in ten- to fifteen-minute episodes that continued over several weeks. All the theaters had a posted charge of 5 cents, but one owner used to stand in front of his theater and ask kids going by how much money they had with them. Even if they had as little as 2 cents he would say, "Gimme it," then let them in.[14]

During the early decades of the twentieth century, the major recreational activity for young adults in Back of the Yards was dancing. Local high schools and churches regularly sponsored dances, and almost every neighborhood tavern had a dance hall behind it. A few large ballrooms attracted young people from across the entire city of Chicago, but the dance craze was largely a local neighborhood phenomenon. Most of the dances in the Yards were organized by the young men's social–athletic clubs. A club would rent a hall and hire a band, and members acted as hosts and bartenders. Sometimes members of the club would arrange a formal entrance for themselves, and with a tumultuous fanfare from the band, the group members would march around the perimeter of the dance floor. Fights among the men were common; sometimes they were over a woman at the dance, and sometimes they resulted from ongoing bad feelings between members of different local clubs. The young women made lengthy preparations for these dances. For example, a typical way to do one's own hair was to roll wet hair around small rolled pieces of newspaper, then tie long strips of cloth through the paper and around the head. When the hair dried and the paper came out, the young woman had a head of curls—an early permanent.[15]

In working-class neighborhoods of large cities across the United States, essentially the same types of locally organized dances were the major form of recreation during the first quarter of the twentieth century. The dances, historian Kathy Peiss notes, were highly provocative for the time, especially in New York but in Chicago and other cities as well. In working-class dance halls around 1900, youths were "pivoting," performing a parody of the stiffly controlled upper-class waltz. The woman stood erect, the man slouched over her, and each put their chins on the other's shoulder. Then they would spin around crazily in tiny circles, in close physical contact, often shouting and singing. Later, working-class youths engaged in "tough dancing": A couple faced each other with pelvises shaking, lowering hands from shoulders to hips and moving closer and closer to each other.[16]

In order to understand fully the place of these dances in enclave social life, let us put the situation of young working-class people from 1910 to 1920 into perspective. Some schooling was valued by immigrant parents, but not necessarily to the point of graduation. In places like Back of the Yards, children as young as 11 years old got jobs in the meat-packing factories or railroad shops. Their strength was more important to employers than their intelligence, and their financial contributions to the household were needed. Parents attempted to control the activities of their working youngsters, and tended to be especially watchful of their daughters whenever a situation even hinted at the possibility of sexual contacts. And in the small, closely knit communities in which they lived, where everyone knew everyone else, one's conduct was almost always subject to surveillance.

Prior to marriage, working-class youths usually lived at home. Neither they nor their parents could afford for them to live in a separate residence, and going off to college was not an alternative. Marriage thus became one of the best means of "liberation." Until at least the late 1950s, many working-class youths, women in particular, married to escape from under the watchful eyes of parents. This escape theme dominated the replies given by working-class women to Mirra Komarovsky's question, "How does marriage change a woman's life?" When many of her respondents described living in their parents' home, they said it had been "like prison" or stated that they had felt "all cooped up." One woman who had married at age 16 offered an additional reason: She wanted to marry to have her own room. She was tired of waiting for her brothers' friends to go home so she could get into her bed, which was in the parlor.[17]

Unmarried women also faced more serious financial problems than men. They earned less on average from paid employment, and those who lived at home ordinarily received less than men in the form of parental "allowances." Almost all young working men and women turned their paychecks over to their parents, and parents in turn gave them some spending money. For women who lived at home, this allowance was typically not enough to pay for much in the way of recreation. An extreme but interesting illustration was provided by W. I. Thomas, a famous member of the old Chicago School of Sociology. One day around 1920, he was collecting information for his research in Chicago's juvenile court when a young girl was brought in for shoplifting. Prior to having stolen some beads and mirrors from a department store, she had worked for two years in a factory. She testified that she had faithfully given her entire $9-per-week pay to her mother, and her mother returned only 10 cents for the girl's own use. Her mother confirmed these facts, which led the judge to resolve the case by directing the mother to increase her daughter's allowance to 25 cents per week.[18]

Women who did not live at home and were self-supporting usually lived in furnished rooms. After paying for room and board, they also had little left over for recreational spending. They often walked to work to save money so they could pay the admission to a dance. It was worth it; a dance was the best place to find excitement and perhaps even meet a prospective husband.

Young men and women typically went to the dance hall with friends of the same sex. Some mixed-sex couples came together on "dates," but that was more common in middle-class circles. When the band began to play, women would often dance with each other. The men would look them over and engage in a practice called "breaking women": Two men would walk up to a pair of dancing women and, with no introductions, separate them, and each man would then dance off with one of the women. The couples might stay together for one dance or for the rest of the evening.[19]

A lot of alcoholic beverages were consumed at the dances. Men drank nickel beers, and a number of cocktails were offered, mostly for the women. The popularity of women in working-class dance halls in Chicago and elsewhere was frequently tied to the amount of alcohol they consumed. Abstainers were ostracized, and sometimes asked to leave, whereas those who drank the most were given prizes. Drinking like this could become expensive, and as already noted, the women had little money. So a woman would hope to find a man who would treat her to drinks. Finding such a man accorded a woman very high status among her peers. In return for treating, however, men ordinarily expected sexual intimacy. It was an arrangement some viewed as bordering on prostitution. From his studies in Chicago, Thomas described these women as an "equivocal class of girls who participate in prostitution without becoming definitely identified with it. The . . . line between the professional and the amateur . . . has become vague."[20]

The habitués of working-class dance halls were often called "charity girls" to differentiate them from prostitutes, who explicitly exchanged sexual participation for money. One New York City vice investigator (in 1917) concluded that the women who regularly frequented certain dance halls were not prostitutes in a legal sense, and he offered the following generalization: "Most . . . are working girls, they smoke cigarettes, drink liquers and dance disorderly dances, and stay out late . . . with any man that pick(s) them up."[21]

CLASS SOLIDARITY AND ETHNIC SUBENCLAVES

Through the first decades of the twentieth century, communities of working-class families were expanding across large sections of cities. In Back of the Yards, for example, employment in meat packing continued to grow, and with the discoveries that waste parts of the slaughtered animals could be used to make a variety of products such as soap and glue, other industries crowded into the Yards. The residential areas housing factory workers grew as a result, producing giant factory towns in the midst of cities. By 1920, Back of the Yards had a population of over 75,000 people, and it blended in with working-class communities of several hundred thousand people on the southwest side of Chicago. Similar working-class aggregations had also formed at the same time in cities such as St. Louis, Philadelphia, and Cleveland.

Even as the spread of the automobile during the 1920s and 1930s made commuting possible for greater numbers of people, factory workers continued to cluster in working-class enclaves. Less-expensive housing was certainly one attraction. Proximity to social–athletic clubs, churches, old friends, and extended families was another. In addition, strong ties between work and community persisted, so people who lived near the factories, whether in Chicago or elsewhere, continued to benefit. In northeast Philadelphia in 1930, for example, there were several hundred thousand people and over 2,000 factories. The largest industries, textiles and metalwork, tended to have seasonal variations in the size of the work force they needed. Workers who were temporarily laid off would seek fill-in jobs at plants that were hiring, but success required personal contacts and knowledge of openings. It depended on "tavern friendships and gossip. . . . Most workers got their jobs because someone they knew 'spoke for them,' or told them on what day to apply at the . . . gate."[22]

During the Great Depression of the 1930s, such contacts were even more important as people struggled to survive. The problems of the entire nation were mirrored in the Back of the Yards: All types of neighborhood retail stores went out of business, all four banks serving the Yards closed at least for a period at one time or another, and many people lost their life savings. Many families had just enough bread and potatoes to eat to stay alive. People foraged for loose boards from railroad tracks that they could burn in their homes as heating fuel.[23] Traditional, community-based forms of informal charity to help people who were temporarily out of work were simply overwhelmed by the sheer number of people who were unemployed. In 1932, almost one-fourth of the civilian labor force was estimated to be unemployed. With homeless people sleeping on courthouse stairs and children starving, such news headlines as "'Girls in High School Bake Cookies for Red Cross Relief' were beginning to look a bit foolish."[24]

Within working-class enclaves, there tended to be an ambivalent attitude toward unions. The C.I.O. (Congress of Industrial Organizations) unions that were organizing workers in the meat-packing, textile, automobile, steel, and other industries tended to be militant and advocate the interests of the workers as a social class. Although only a minority of union leaders were avowed Marxists seeking revolutionary changes, many others held with a Marxist-inspired view that emphasized the similarities among all wage workers in their relations to the means of production. Many of the workers, however, were first- and second-generation immigrants "who remained embedded in a culture defined by traditional ties to family, kinship, church, and neighborhood club or tavern."[25] In other words, their identities were bound up in their ties to neighborhood institutions more than in membership in a broader, more inclusive class as advocated by unions.

In addition, different ethnic groups were often in competition with each other over the same factory jobs and places to live. They focused their efforts on keeping members of other ethnic groups out of their jobs and their neighborhoods. This competition reinforced interethnic hostilities.

The growth of the union movement, on the other hand, required that workers regard class struggle as more important than their interethnic conflicts.[26]

The hardships of the Great Depression slowly led many blue-collar workers to conclude that their traditional relationship with industry, which did not include unions, could no longer be sustained. In addition to the workers' shift in attitude, and to substantial long-term effect, leaders of the trade union movement realized that the success of the movement depended on unions' ability to forge links to local working-class enclaves. They recognized that community support was critical to a union's chances of organizing workers. Thus, in Back of the Yards during the 1930s, the Packinghouse Workers Unions engaged in such activities as raising funds for local orphanages and sponsoring youth activities, and union leaders attended neighborhood housing meetings.

It was in conjunction with initial efforts to combat juvenile delinquency in the Yards that local church and union leadership created the Back of the Yards Neighborhood Council in 1939. The council firmly linked factory, union, and community. Its very first resolution called on the Armour meat-packing company to meet union demands in order to avert a strike that would harm the community. Later, it urged all union members to shop exclusively at stores within the Yards.[27]

By the middle of the twentieth century the Neighborhood Council had slowly enveloped most of the different enclaves within Back of the Yards, forging ties across different ethnic groups and church organizations. The Yards became more of a single community centering around a common class and less a series of separate ethnic villages, although many remnants of the latter remained. In sum, working-class identity and union membership transcended, without replacing, ethnic boundaries. The ethnic enclaves that persisted might better be described as subenclaves.

THE DECLINE OF WORKING-CLASS ENCLAVES

The trend toward more inclusive communities based on class rather than ethnicity was paradoxically occurring at the same time that factories started to move out of established working-class communities. In Chicago, most of the meat packers began to leave the stockyards area during the 1950s. Like most U.S. factories involved in the same kind of exodus, they moved from North to South, from East to West, from cities to small towns, and sometimes completely out of the country.

For a variety of reasons, working-class enclaves have not typically formed around the relocated factories. The work force of IBP Inc., a major food-processing company, is illustrative. In 1980, IBP moved to Garden City, a small town in southwest Kansas. Over the next decade the company hired nearly 3,000 people. Some workers came from the area, others came from Iowa and Nebraska, but the bulk of the work force now consists of relatively new immigrants from Asia or South America.

Garden City is not the initial (or final) destination of these immigrants. They move to Garden City from Los Angeles and other large Western cities in response to work opportunities and a chance for a better life. They do not, however, typically remain in Garden City for very long. They accumulate a little money, then head for Texas or Louisiana in search of other kinds of work or to start their own businesses. They do not form enclaves, as we have employed the term, for a variety of reasons, beginning with the fact that they have a very weak place attachment. The outlook of Bob Ma, a Vietnamese refugee, is illustrative. He met his Chicana wife in Los Angeles, where he had made a marginal living in construction. After moving to Kansas and working for six months at IBP, Inc., he and his wife bought a trailer to live in. He explains, "Over there, in L.A., it's too wild and expensive. Over here, it's boring, but it's better. And you don't got to stay forever. You can save up and move on."[28]

The working-class enclaves of the Northern cities deserted by factories have suffered a number of different fates. Many became slums very quickly, as home owners who feared for the future of their neighborhoods were panicked into selling their houses for whatever they could get. Land speculators bought the homes and converted them to accommodate multiple families. Housing prices then fell further, there was more panic selling, and the spiral continued. This familiar process of deterioration was at work in Back of the Yards when the Neighborhood Council (which had survived the exodus of the factories) succeeded in getting banks to invest in the area, in encouraging families who remained to remodel their homes, and in sponsoring a new housing development that succeeded in attracting new families. By the late 1960s, housing values in the Yards actually began to increase, and portions of the Yards were preserved as part of a stable residential area.[29]

With the stockyards gone, Back of the Yards is a less meaningful geographic area. Today this historic area is often considered a part of adjacent neighborhoods from which it had historically been separate. Most of the factories once found in this community and much of the way of life that had evolved around them are gone. However, while many of the countries of origin have changed, people continue to come to this area and live in communities that possess many of the characteristics of ethnic enclaves (or subenclaves). Today they include Polish, Hispanic, and Chinese residents. In the community newspaper, Anna Nowobilska, M.D., advertises health care services for the entire family, and her ads include the note, "Dr. Nowobilska speaks fluent English and Polish." A three-person general dental office located a few blocks away emphasizes the same quality, in Polish: "Mowimy Po Polsku." LaPalma Supermarket, which carries imported brands of coffee, beans, and other distinctive products for a Hispanic clientele, presents part of its newspaper advertisements in Spanish. Realtors such as Century 21 who attempt to bridge the separate enclaves proudly advertise, "We speak Polish, Spanish and Chinese."[30]

The ethnic enclaves continue to be focused around local parishes, but these parishes are less closed to outsiders than they used to be. They actually compete with each other to attract people from the extended community to their bingo nights. St. Bruno Parish's newspaper advertisements promise a free card and bonus ball every Friday night; St. Maurice's Monday-night bingo offers a $500 Coverall; and, not to be outdone, St. Barbara Parish promises Thursday-night bingo with an early bird special, a birthday club, two $500 games and the "best bingo that can be found!"[31]

There also remains a mixture of ethnic animosity and working-class solidarity in the community that mirrors its past. On the one hand, apparently concerned with increasing numbers of people of color in the neighborhood, one conspicuously Polish writer took out an advertisement in the community newspaper condemning the government's laxity in enforcing immigration laws. He claimed the cost of supporting illegals in U.S. prisons to be $800 million yearly and urged readers to write their representatives. On the other hand, issues such as trade and tariff agreements with other nations tend to transcend differences in race and ethnicity, inspiring working-class cohesion. Chicago factory workers who have kept their jobs or are trying to replace jobs they lost emphasize class considerations in discussing such issues. For example, one referred to the people who preferred free trade with Mexico and Canada as "fancy pants elites" who do not care about American workers' jobs. He concluded, "I guess when you live up on a hill, you just don't see the people in the valley."[32]

The people who remain in working-class enclaves or subenclaves after the factories leave obviously have to find other kinds of employment, and this is both practically and emotionally difficult. In ethnic and working-class South Philadelphia, for example, nearly 50,000 people were once employed as welders, installers, and other such workers at the Naval Shipyard. The Shipyard is scheduled to close before the year 2000, however, and with the Philadelphia area losing over 7,500 manufacturing jobs yearly during the 1990s, it is unlikely that many in this community will find similar kinds of new jobs. As part of a federal retraining program, thousands of shipyard workers are now studying to be respiratory therapists, hairdressers, medical technicians, real estate agents, and paralegals. Even if they remain in the shipyard area, however, the nature of the residential community will not be the same. As one long-time resident explained, "When you talk about the shipyard you're not just talking about a job, you're talking about a choice of life."[33]

NOTES

1. For a detailed description of Philadelphia during this period, see Sam B. Warner, Jr., *The Private City,* Philadelphia: University of Pennsylvania Press, 1968.

2. William Cronon, *Nature's Metropolis,* New York: W. W. Norton, 1991.

3. Dominic A. Pacyga, *Polish Immigrants and Industrial Chicago,* Columbus: Ohio State University Press, 1991.

4. Milton B. Hunt, "The Housing of Non-Family Groups of Men in Chicago," *American Journal of Sociology* 16, 1910.

5. Robert A. Slayton, *Back of the Yards,* Chicago: University of Chicago Press, 1986, p. 74.

6. Sophonisba P. Breckinridge and Edith Abbott, "Chicago's Housing Problem: Families in Furnished Rooms," *American Journal of Sociology* 16, 1910.

7. Thomas J. Jablonsky, *Pride in the Jungle,* Baltimore: The Johns Hopkins University Press, 1993.

8. Slayton, op. cit.

9. Charles J. Bushnell, "Some Social Aspects of the Chicago Stock Yards," *American Journal of Sociology* 7, 1901, p. 301. For more examples of the humanitarian and welfare emphasis of many of the Chicago dissertations of this time, see Robert E. L. Faris, *Chicago Sociology,* San Francisco: Chandler, 1967.

10. Pacyga, op. cit.

11. Slayton, op. cit., p. 112.

12. Pacyga, op. cit.

13. Slayton, op. cit.

14. Slayton, op. cit., p. 59.

15. Ibid., p. 61.

16. Kathy Peiss, "Dance Madness: New York City Dance Halls and Working-Class Sexuality, 1900–1920," in Charles Stephenson and Robert Asher (Eds.), *Life and Labor: Dimensions of American Working-Class History,* Albany: State University of New York Press, 1986.

17. Mirra Komarovsky, *Blue Collar World,* New Haven, CT: Yale University Press, 1987 (originally published in 1962).

18. W. I. Thomas, *The Unadjusted Girl,* New York: Harper & Row, 1967, p. 108 (originally published in 1923).

19. Peiss, op. cit.

20. Thomas, op. cit., p. 119.

21. Peiss, op. cit., p. 187.

22. Warner, op. cit., p. 181.

23. Slayton, op. cit.

24. Robert S. Lynd and Helen M. Lynd, *Middletown in Transition,* New York: Harcourt, Brace, 1937, p. 106.
25. Melvyn Dubofsky, "Not So 'Turbulent Years': A New Look at the 1930s," in Stephenson and Asher, op. cit.
26. For further discussion, see Suzan Olzak, "Labor Unrest, Immigration, and Ethnic Conflict in America, 1880–1914," *American Journal of Sociology* 94, 1989.
27. Slayton, op. cit.
28. Quoted in *The New York Times,* October 18, 1993, p. B7.
29. Slayton, op. cit.
30. Advertisements from the *Brighton Park and McKinley Park Life,* November 4, 1993.
31. Ibid. Essentially the same advertisements appear most weeks.
32. Quoted in *The New York Times,* November 14, 1993, p. 16.
33. Quoted in *The New York Times,* October 17, 1993, p. 18.

4

African Americans in Detroit

On the downtown waterfront of Detroit stands the Renaissance Center (locally called "the RenCen"). It is a modern, seventy-three-story hotel, office tower, and convention center as well as a shopping mall with four movie theaters and thirteen restaurants. For those who come by car, expressways make the RenCen highly accessible, although newcomers are usually a bit overwhelmed when they first enter the building and confront a battery of elevators, escalators, and spiral staircases. For those who have business to transact, the Center offers cushioned seats by ponds and waterfalls and cocktail lounges with dangling greenery. Its lobbies are full of well-dressed conventioneers and local businesspeople.

Across the expressway that runs in front of the RenCen, then down a few streets is inner-city Detroit. The area contains block after block of abandoned, burned cottages on weedy plots, gutted apartment buildings, and boarded-up little stores. On a windy day, dirt and discarded newspapers swirl down deserted streets. Interspersed among the abandoned structures are dilapidated, but occupied, houses where bunches of young children play on broken-down porches. There are a few large public housing projects, and here and there an empty factory, a reminder of the city that Detroit used to be.[1]

The busy expressway is a barrier to anyone in the inner city who might want to walk over to the RenCen. For local residents who manage to cross the expressway, access is also discouraged by an entrance that is surprisingly difficult for pedestrians to see because it is recessed and largely hidden behind a concrete rampart. In addition, a very large and visible security staff patrols the entire complex and monitors its entrance.

Some of the city's burned and deserted buildings are a remnant of the uncontrolled fires in the rioting of 1967. During the middle 1960s there were large-scale inner-city riots in many cities with large African American populations, such as New York, Chicago, Cleveland, and Los Angeles. The largest of those riots was in Detroit, where police and federal troops engaged in sporadic gun battles with armed residents over the period of a week. Meanwhile, arsonists and looters celebrated in the streets in the light

49

of huge fires that gutted hundreds of stores and shops. When it was over, many sections of the inner city resembled a devastated war zone.[2]

The destruction of inner-city stores and buildings that began in the 1967 riot continued during the 1980s, when the night before Halloween came to be known locally as "Devil's Night," which was celebrated by burn-ing dozens of structures, mostly in the inner city. One Devil's Night spectator recalled that the scent of burning wood and the sight of large fires surrounded by hundreds of onlookers initially reminded him of a home-coming rally. However, that light-hearted impression vanished when he noticed the grim looks on the faces of neighbors, mostly older African Americans, who stood in front of their homes with coats over their bathrobes. They held shotguns and garden hoses to protect their property while the police guarded the overextended fire fighters.[3]

Detroit's most visible renewal effort resulted in the RenCen complex; but it has not been financially successful, nor has it stimulated the reju-venation of the center of Detroit that some backers had hoped would occur. A trolley covers a one-mile route from the RenCen through down-town, and passengers who wish to can get off near park benches that mark the end of the line. Two elderly women, "visitors" from Detroit's suburbs, got off one day. As the trolley left, they looked fearfully at the empty buildings and deserted streets at the edge of the downtown area. A Wayne State professor happened to walk by, and one of the women asked him what he thought they should do. He suggested they walk around or sit on the benches and wait for the trolley to return. "But won't we be killed?" she asked.[4]

While Devil's Night was becoming an annual tradition in Detroit, shootings among its citizens were becoming an everyday event. The city's rate of violent crime continued to rise during the 1980s, leading the state legislature to consider gun control proposals; but Coleman Young, Detroit's African American mayor, refused to support any measure that would impose gun control in the city. He said he did not want to "disarm Detroit" as long as the city was surrounded by "hostile suburbs" and armed Ku Klux Klan "vigilantes."[5] To people unfamiliar with race relations in Detroit, Mayor Young's position may have been impossible to under-stand, but it stems from the fact that African Americans in Detroit have frequently been the victims of mob violence.

EARLY HISTORY

It was around 1850 that Detroit changed from a small frontier town to a manufacturing center. During the following decades the city grew, as Southerners and European immigrants came to find work. Shipbuilding and other types of manufacturing used the Detroit River, and because most people had to walk to work the areas closest to the river grew first.

The unpaved streets of the east riverfront were home to a dense mixture of stores, factories, and the one- and two-story frame houses of immigrants. Around 1860, estimates indicated that Detroit's African American population had increased to over 1,000 persons, 80 percent of whom were clustered among immigrant populations on Detroit's near east side. The streets with higher concentrations of African Americans tended to be referred to as "Negro Areas," but analysis of city directories suggests that there was no one street in the city on which African Americans comprised 50 percent or more of the residents. Most African Americans lived in areas with mixed immigrant populations, though they tended to live in the oldest, smallest apartments.[6]

Because Blacks, Southern whites, and European immigrants competed for jobs and for housing, relations between these groups could be particularly hostile. The crowded, integrated, near east side "erupted" in 1863 when an African American man was accused of sexually assaulting two 9-year-old girls, one black and the other white. The girls later confessed they had made up the entire story, but not before the man was found guilty and sentenced to life in prison. As soldiers were escorting him to the prison, a crowd of African Americans threw stones and bricks at them and tried to seize the prisoner. The soldiers fired several volleys, wounding and killing some in the crowd. They were then able to move the prisoner into the jail, and they returned to their barracks, thinking the incident over. However, a white mob, comprising mostly immigrants, then formed and went on a haphazard spree, setting fire to the homes of African Americans. Following the rules set by the Detroit fire marshall, only when white homes were accidentally set ablaze did the fire department turn on their hoses. Shouting "Kill the nigger!" white men and boys also clubbed and beat any blacks they happened to find on the street.

Within a period of about six months, in the spring and summer of 1863, white mobs went on similar rampages in other Northern cities. Competition among groups living in crowded, integrated communities was the common underlying cause. The worst of the riots, in terms of total death toll, probably occurred in New York when drunken immigrants stormed into the city's African American sections, burning homes, looting stores, and hanging people from lampposts.[7]

When electric streetcars were installed in Detroit in the 1880s, they enabled people to commute to work from longer distances, and the city's growing white population expanded outward. However, the growing African American population remained mostly concentrated in the near east side. Between 1880 and 1910 the city of Detroit grew from just over 100,000 persons to nearly half a million. The African American population doubled during this period, reaching a total of nearly 6,000 persons.

Throughout these decades, about 85 percent of the city's African American population lived in the near east side.[8] Other ethnic groups also lived there: a large German population resided in a section called "Little Berlin," and there were also substantial numbers of Irish, Polish, and Jewish immigrant groups. Nevertheless, it was in the near east side that Detroit's most complete African American enclave formed in the early twentieth century.

THE NEAR-EAST-SIDE ENCLAVE

Let us begin by identifying this area of Detroit's near east side on a map. Woodward Avenue, in the center, was a wide, tree-lined boulevard with mansions and small private homes. It was Detroit's principal north–south thoroughfare, dissecting the city into east and west sides. When the electric streetcars enabled the east-side population to expand, the heaviest suburban-type concentrations remained near Woodward. The near east side refers to the area east of Woodward, between Gratiot and the river.

In Detroit's near east side around 1910, there were variations in the wealth of African Americans that correlated with how recently they had moved to Detroit and where in the near east side they lived. The waterfront area contained rooming houses that were home to the poor and disabled, the disreputable (such as criminals and alcoholics), and young newcomers to Detroit. At the opposite, northern, end of the near east side, close to Gratiot, was situated a small African American middle and upper class, composed of owners of small shops, salesmen, and the like. They lived in small cottages that they owned.

Most African American families in the near east side were, both physically and socially, between the two extremes. They lived in apartments that varied from poor to horrible. There were a large number of one- and two-story wooden frame homes, sometimes separate and sometimes built in rows. Each floor was subdivided into a number of small apartments, but because African Americans paid a premium for any kind of housing, they were under pressure to sublet some of their already limited space to other tenants. Thus, these old, deteriorating cottages were very crowded. A number of African American families also lived in the upper floors of three-story brick buildings, above barbershops, saloons, drugstores, or restaurants. Rear entrances led to these upstairs apartments, which were very small and dark. (The sides of the buildings had no windows so that new buildings could easily be attached to them.) Many of the poorest black families lived in sheds and stables, located in alleys, that had been converted to rows of family dwellings. Alleys had been built behind the streets in the near east side, originally to provide access to stables and for sewerage systems, later for use as garbage-dumping grounds. Naturally, they presented serious health hazards

Detroit's Near East Side

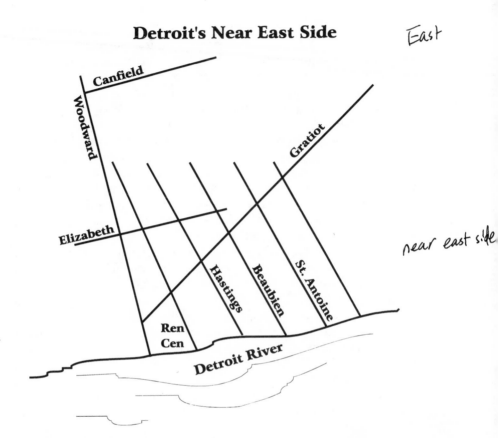

for residents. Most of the alley dwellings were unpainted wooden units, less than six feet wide, but many of the residents still took in boarders.[9]

A majority of the African American families in the near east side could probably best be described as struggling members of the lower working class. Most took whatever kind of work they could find, but they often could not find enough to be continuously employed. Their ongoing job searches, and the African American newcomers' ignorance of city ways, led to a good deal of harassment by whites in the guise of humor. For example, bogus work orders for day labor were given to black men, who would show up for work at the designated place only to discover that the contractor did not exist.

White-owned stores outside of the area frequently refused service to African American customers or tried to discourage their business. Many middle-class, white-owned restaurants and hotels employed African Americans but, even so, refused to serve them or required that they pay double if they insisted on going where they were not wanted. White barbers typically refused to cut the hair of African Americans, citing fear that it would drive away their white customers. Ironically, many African American barbers with white clienteles expressed the same fear and refused to cut the hair of other African Americans. Thus blacks who opened restaurants or barbershops in the near east side found a concentrated number of ready patrons; so too did those who opened such businesses as drugstores, funeral parlors, taverns, and pool halls. By 1910 St. Antoine Street was the commercial center of the African American community.

The capital for this commerce came in large part from real estate and related investments. There were a number of free blacks who had migrated from Virginia to Detroit before the Civil War, and they had brought with them funds that they used to buy a good deal of land. That land lay in what later became the downtown business district and in the near east side. Later, other African American businessmen and professionals also invested in land, mostly in the near east side. Then, as the black business district expanded northward up St. Antoine, the value of real estate holdings increased dramatically, producing capital for further commercial and residential expansion. In addition, some rental housing in the near east side was owned by African Americans, and there were several prominent African American real estate agents and promoters. The African American land owners and promoters maintained the east-of-Woodward color line because they benefitted economically from keeping the growing black population in the crowded near east side.[10]

The St. Antoine commercial district was a place in which African Americans were welcome as customers. Leaders of their community urged them to patronize African American businesses as a matter of racial pride. It was also the area in which goods and services distinctively associated with the African American community were readily available: products for straightening hair and whitening skin; "soul" food, such as fatback, collards, and chitterlings; and newspapers published by African Americans that focused on issues of interest to African American readers. The shared cultural traditions of those who had come to Detroit from the South were also kept alive in "back-alley jukes" behind Hastings Street and in waterfront saloons, where African American musicians played and sang the blues. These were mostly small, raucous nightclubs that featured the blues and bawdy humor, and sometimes had brothels and gambling as well. Some clubs had an almost exclusively black, male laborer clientele from the immediate area; others catered to more varied audiences.

One of the better-known performers at Hastings Street clubs around 1910 was Speckled Red, later known as Detroit Red. He performed in African American clubs in cities throughout the Midwest and in traveling medicine shows throughout the South. Red's most famous song, "The Dirty Dozens," was originally a rhyme used to teach children the biblical creation story. As a blues number, it evolved into an obscene series of verbal insults, culminating in the accusation, explicitly stated, that a man had had intercourse with his own mother.[11] (The strong language and graphic sexual descriptions of these early black performers has continued through contemporary hip-hop-rap, an African American cultural form initially limited primarily to inner-city neighborhoods.)[12]

Most of the blues as played and sung in these clubs was created by African Americans to make sense out of lives and events that often made no sense. It was a musical form that provided an emotional commentary on the misfortunes of people living poor and black. "Going Down the Road, Feelin' Bad," for example, recounts the days of the "man snatchers" in the old South. These were agents employed by cotton farmers or railroad supervisors who needed laborers. The man snatchers would get African American men drunk and cart them off. The hijacked men would then find themselves miles from home, with no alternative to working as laborers. When they finished working, however, there would usually be no pay, and they had to trudge back home empty-handed.[13]

Churches were another major institution in the cultural life of the near east side. In the rural South, family and church had been the primary institutions, and African Americans' reverence for them was carried to the Northern cities. Outside of the home, the church was the only place where blacks had status and were not subordinate to whites. The pastor/preacher/minister was the leading figure in, and the church was the organizational center for, the African American community. Newcomers to the city often first turned to the older, established Baptist and Methodist churches for help in finding work and shelter. However, the number of migrants began to increase dramatically during the first decades of the twentieth century, and they overwhelmed the traditional churches' capacities.

A large number of new African American churches were born in the crowded streets of Detroit's near east side. A few were large, having been explicitly built as churches, and attracted citywide followings. Most, however, were small—converted storefronts and residences—and they served a very local area, mirroring the small and intimate African American church of the South. A typical example was the Holiness Church of Living God, founded by "Bishop" J. B. C. Cummings. He began organizing his "brethren and sistern" in the near east side, and in 1909 he bought a small frame house off Beaubien Street and put up a banner, and his "temple" was in operation.[14]

This proliferation of local congregations was an attempt to establish within the city the kind of institution with which the recent migrants were familiar. They were comfortable with a church in which if someone were not in their usual seat on a Sunday, the pastor would come to their home to find out what was wrong. By contrast, the large denominational churches were bureaucratic and impersonal, and in the white denominational churches, blacks were relegated to the rear. The small storefront churches also offered forms of worship with which the migrants were accustomed: familiar spirituals and hymns; and singing, shouting, dancing, and other forms of free religious expression.[15]

Of particular significance in Detroit and elsewhere during the early decades of the twentieth century was the Black Spiritual Movement. Many of its congregations were nominally identified as Baptist, but were actually amalgams of diverse practices and beliefs, with elements taken from such practices as Catholicism, Pentacostalism, Spiritualism, Judaism, and Voodoo. For example, the leader of the Spiritual Israel Church in Detroit has the title of Bishop, is regarded by members as "king of Israel," and is addressed as "holy father." In addition to the minister (or king or queen), the major roles found in many spiritual churches include the following:

> **Missionaries:** women who may say a prayer or give a short sermon during Sunday services and help the sick or needy during the week.
>
> **Mothers:** older women who may assist in the service and have been accorded a place of honor in a reserved section of pews.
>
> **Mediums:** men or women with the gift of prophecy who are also known as prophets or spiritual advisors. During services they provide "messages" to many congregants, and in private they offer advice about everyday life, sometimes suggesting what numbers a person should bet on in policy games or lotteries. Many are also believed to be healers.
>
> **Nurses:** usually women dressed like hospital nurses, stationed throughout the sanctuary. During services they look after congregants who collapse or fall into trances.[16]

In summation, let us consider the degree to which the African American population of Detroit's near east side constituted an enclave. The primary question is whether a distinct group occupies a clearly defined area. While the near east side was also home to nonblacks, the sheer presence of "outsiders" does not negate an enclave. The crux of the matter is whether the concentration was sufficient for it to be regarded as an African American area, and it was. It is also apparent that the distinct group's way of life was supported by specialized local institutions and commercial activities. The enclave characteristic we know least about in this case concerns whether the African American residents felt an attachment to the near east side. Many probably did. Housing, employment opportunities, and harassment were worse in the South they had left behind, and the near east side housed the churches, clubs, products, family, and friends that were integral to their collective lives. Thus in 1910 in Detroit's near east side, the concentration of African Americans probably qualified as an enclave. In this regard it differs from the contemporary African American ghetto in Detroit and those elsewhere. Some of the differences and their implications are discussed later in this chapter.

A SUBURBAN-TYPE NEAR-ENCLAVE

An African American upper class, living in mansions located in predominantly white areas or in distinct sections of larger black areas, emerged after about 1880 in Boston, Chicago, New Orleans, and a number of other cities, including Detroit. A large percentage of the African American upper class in Detroit were offspring of the prominent "free black" (nonslave) families that had migrated to Detroit from Virginia before the Civil War. Many of these original families were well educated by the standards of their day, and they brought business skills, capital, and a strong work ethic with them to Detroit. Only about 10 percent of all blacks were free prior to the Civil War, but the material and nonmaterial advantages of this group were transmitted from generation to generation for over 100 years. In the 1960s, for example, over 50 percent of black professionals surveyed were found to be descendants of free African American ancestors.[17]

Along with a few relative newcomers, the grown children of the free blacks from Virginia formed an exclusive social clique initially consisting of forty families, which they called the "cultured, colored forty." Between 1900 and 1910 the group actually grew to include fifty-one families that constituted the core of the African American upper class in Detroit. Within this clique were six physicians, seven attorneys, and three dentists, many of whom had substantial white clienteles. Nonprofessionals were also included in the city's black aristocracy if they had family ties to members of the aristocracy, or they had substantial wealth, typically gained from inner-city real estate investments.

Formal social activities such as dances, dinners, and teas were usually held in the clique's large and well-furnished homes. Only other clique members were regularly included on guest lists. (There were a number of other upper-status African American families that were a little less prominent or a little less rich that were included only periodically.) Except for the summer months, when the families vacationed in Saratoga Springs, their social calendars were full. Teenage children were included in the formal activities of Detroit's upper-class African Americans. The youngsters mingled, their parents nearby to serve as chaperons, and gradually learned the genteel ways of behaving expected in "polite society."[18]

A majority of the upper-class African American families lived between Woodward and St. Antoine well north of Gratiot, where streetcars had facilitated the development of suburban-type residential areas in the city. Here they lived on tree-lined streets, in well-tended three-story homes bordered by privet hedges. A few upper-class families lived on streets just off Gratiot, and there were at least some who lived in mansions west of Woodward, where they were the only black families in their neighborhoods.

The most important associations and institutions of the upper class tended to be located near the area of its greatest concentration. For example, the Phillis Wheatley Association was an organization of elite African American women whose major charitable activity was the Home for Aged Colored Ladies. This voluntary association's headquarters was an eleven-room house on Elizabeth Street. Also on Elizabeth was the St. Matthew's Protestant Episcopal Mission, the church to which nearly two-thirds of the fifty-one *most* elite African American families belonged, and which families comprised the church's governing core.[19]

When St. Matthew's was first established in 1846, it was the first black Episcopal church west of the Alleghenies. In those early years, however, it was too small to be viable, and a decade later black Episcopalians sought baptisms and confirmations in white churches. In 1883 a new building was erected on Elizabeth Street, and the pulpit was given over to a succession of mostly white ministers. After 1890, a series of distinguished African American clergy were brought in, and the parish grew to over 500 communicants by 1920.[20] Unlike other African American churches in Detroit, St. Matthew's recruited a lot of its membership from beyond its immediate neighborhood. Even so, the church's pew rental policy kept out poor newcomers, who probably would not have been attracted to its dignified and reserved services in any case. To most of the elite membership, it seemed entirely reasonable for poor blacks to worship in separate churches. Rich and poor blacks, they believed, were two groups that had "nothing in common."[21]

Questions about the proper relationship between the small African American upper class and the much larger African American lower class were frequently raised in response to the upper-class women's "self-culture" clubs. In cities across the country, upper-class African American women met regularly to study literature, art, and music. Their highly restrictive clubs emulated those of the white upper class, and were designed to help mold the "ideal lady": cultured, fashionable, confident. It is easy to understand why such women might have seemed haughty, and their concern with matters of style absurd, to lower-class African Americans. At the same time, the women's clubs did periodically involve themselves in some matters of more general racial concern, such as antilynching crusades and support for local orphanages. At any rate, not all upper-class women, black or white, subscribed to this notion of the "ideal lady." Some pursued professions and were highly successful. Meta Pelham, for example, ran a family-owned newspaper, and a number of other women's club members served actively on a variety of Detroit's civic boards.[22]

Members of the African American elite were also divided on questions of racial integration. Those who justified a clear separation between themselves and poor African Americans tended to see integration as the ideal and to believe that it was attainable. This segment of the elite included physicians and lawyers with predominantly white clienteles, and others who participated in elite black clubs while belonging to predominantly white churches.

In evaluating this group on its enclave characteristics, one notes first that the African American upper class was a distinctive group whose lifestyle was supported by special institutions. However, even though most of the elite families lived in eastern streetcar suburbs, where their local organizations and associations were located as well, they were too small a part of the overall area to have given it an African American identity. Furthermore, if the area were predominantly African American, regardless of class, it is not clear that most of the elite would have felt the same attachment to the place. Thus the term "near-enclave" fits best, because although the African American upper class was a very distinctive group, and most of its members lived in the same area, neither racial nor territorial identities seemed sufficiently strong to warrant the enclave label.

Over the next few decades, most of the signs of this near-enclave disappeared. The traditional, distinctively local upper classes in all cities were declining, among both African Americans and whites, as described in Chapter Two. In addition, and more specific to Detroit, some of the elite African American families were childless. The offspring of other families moved to cities such as Chicago and Washington, where the African American upper class was considerably larger. So Detroit's African American elite, small to begin with, grew too small to constitute even a near-enclave.

What became of the larger enclave in the near east side is a more complex story. Despite the black population's continued growth and segregation from whites, that enclave also disappeared. We close this chapter with an examination of how the enclave eventually became the victim of a redevelopment plan, and why a new enclave did not form in its place.

MORE GROWTH, MORE SEGREGATION

During the first half of the twentieth century, there was a steady stream of migration into Detroit from Arkansas, Kentucky, Alabama, and Tennessee, where job opportunities were very limited. Around the onset of both world wars (1917 and 1941), jobs created in relation to war-related factory production led to peaks in the migration rates. In both instances, the influx of job-seeking migrants overwhelmed the supply of housing, competition for housing between whites and blacks intensified, and blacks were left more segregated than before. Several dramatic confrontations symbolized the degree of white opposition to integration.

During the first peak, what had been small Ku Klux Klan chapters in Detroit grew as a result of both the influx of Southern whites and a national "Klan fever" following the success of the 1915 film *The Birth of a Nation*. That movie presented a sympathetic portrayal of the klansman as noble white hero, and led to popular emulation of klan dress, in costume parties, for example.[23] A rejuvenated Klan in Detroit reached out to the white immigrant Europeans, teaching them whom Americans were supposed to hate. "Using the odious term 'niggers' gave the foreign-born worker (mainly Polish) a sense of identity with white society."[24]

Even high-status African Americans found it difficult to find suitable places to live, because most of the white population was disinclined to make socioeconomic distinctions among African Americans. The case of Ossian Sweet, a physician, is illustrative. In 1925, when Dr. Sweet and his wife (also a college graduate) bought a home in a formerly all-white neighborhood, the Klan in Detroit organized opposition. The police ignored groups of whites who milled nightly across the street, throwing stones at the Sweets's house. One night someone in the home shot into the crowd, killing one white man and injuring another. Then the police responded, arresting the Sweets along with his brother (a dentist) and several other family members who were in the home at the time. A long series of trials began, during which time Klan membership and influence increased. The mayor, who was considered liberal and had strong African American backing, nevertheless condemned the Sweets and others who would follow in their footsteps. In his open letter to a Detroit newspaper in 1925, he wrote, "I must say that I depreciate most strongly the moving of Negroes or other persons into districts in which they know their presence may cause riots of bloodshed."[25]

Over the next decades Detroit's growing African American population continued, for the most part, to reside in terribly substandard housing on the east side. When migration dramatically accelerated around 1940, though, the housing problem became too serious to ignore. In order to house war workers, agencies of the federal government decided in 1941 to fund two projects through the Detroit Housing Commission. The Commission planned to build one housing project of several hundred units for blacks on the east side (named Sojourner Truth Homes after the Civil War poet) and one for whites in a white area. The site for the proposed African American project was later moved west, to a white area, despite protests from the local residents. After the project was completed and leases were signed, the Ku Klux Klan organized picket lines of over 1,000 men, many of whom were armed, to prevent the new tenants from actually entering. For several days at the end of February 1942, small groups of African Americans tried to drive through the barricade but were forced to retreat under a barrage of bricks. On March 1st the fighting escalated, and about twenty people, black and white, required hospitalization to treat wounds caused by knives, bullets, and flying bricks. Police subsequently arrested participants on such charges as inciting to riot, assault, and carrying concealed weapons. Of the 104 arrested, 102 were black.[26]

In the postwar years the suburbs outside of Detroit grew rapidly, but African Americans were largely excluded from them. The most violence tended to occur when African Americans tried to integrate ethnic, blue-collar suburbs such as Dearborn. In this suburb just west of the city, near Ford's River Rouge plant, there were a number of mob actions during the 1950s and 1960s. The regularly reelected mayor of Dearborn, Orville Hubbard, opposed integration on the grounds that it would lead to racial intermarriage and "mongrelization." The Dearborn police called on any African American family that moved into town and suggested they move out as quickly as possible. When they stayed and white mobs threw bottles and bricks, the Dearborn police failed to take any action.[27] In upper-class suburbs, in contrast, African Americans were typically excluded by more subtle means, because white homeowners feared that violent demonstrations would harm neighborhood reputations and, therefore, property values.

During the period of Detroit's rapid suburban growth, roughly from 1950 to 1980, fifty incorporated communities were added to the metropolitan area. These villages and townships, which became the new suburbs, contained a total of nearly three-quarters of a million white people and fewer than 5,000 African Americans; less than 1 percent of the population of the new suburbs was African American.[28] Among the large U.S. metropolitan areas in 1990, Detroit's was the most racially segregated.[29]

When African Americans did move out of the city, it was usually into older suburban areas. Realtors regularly profited from this movement by "block busting." Using fear of invasion by blacks to spur white residents to sell at any price, realtors would buy property cheap, then sell it at high prices to black families or partition it into smaller units for rent. Meanwhile, white neighbors were stampeded into selling at further-reduced prices, and agents made off with the bargains. One block at a time, the African American ghetto spread, following on the heels of middle-class African Americans trying to move up and out. One long-term consequence is that among African Americans there is now almost no correlation between their social class and the racial segregation of their neighborhoods. To be specific, African Americans in Detroit making over

$50,000 per year are about as segregated as those making less than $2,500; both live in almost totally segregated areas. In contrast, as the income level of Asians or Hispanics rises, their levels of segregation from whites drop by about 25 percent.[30]

THE DEMISE OF THE ENCLAVE

By midcentury, parts of the inner cores of many industrial cities, including Detroit, were so old and deteriorated that their market values had steeply declined. The low value of inner-city parcels of land made redevelopment, or "slum clearance" attractive to entrepreneurs. City officials were often convinced to take the side of the entrepreneurs by the belief that redevelopment would lower crime or increase tax revenues. For these postwar redevelopment plans to be eligible for federal funds, however, the city had to provide other housing for the people who were displaced. Beginning around 1950, public housing projects were touted as the answer. In principle, they were cost-effective ways to address the housing shortage and meet federal requirements, but in reality, they almost never fully replaced the lost housing.

Urban renewal, sociologist Gerald Suttles argues, has generally tended to proceed like a successful "confidence game." Announcement of the plan is usually made in a setting that commands attention, such as the mayor's office or a penthouse executive suite. Scale models are presented to give the public the sense that the project is solid, real. It is often claimed that the improvements will occur at no cost to the city; funds will come only from the private sector or the federal government. Furthermore, if the project is begun at once, a front man promises, jobs will be created and the neighborhood will receive, as an additional free gift, a park or a plaza. Any delays, on the other hand, could result in cost overruns that would jeopardize the entire project. Thus the plan moves forward like a steamroller over the objections of residents who do not wish to be displaced.[31]

The first and largest site selected for redevelopment in Detroit was a 129-acre portion of Hastings Street, south of Gratiot—a deteriorated section near the center of the 1910 enclave. During the early 1950s hundreds of resident families were forced to vacate their dwellings after receiving official notification that demolition was imminent, but it did not occur for ten more years. Most resettled close to their original homes while the city's plans were debated over the next decade. Low-income (replacement) housing was eventually built in the original enclave area and just to the east of it, forcing many of these families to move again.[32] Then one high-rise project after another was built in the inner city.

factories moved out

lose jobs

At the same time that it was experiencing a proliferation of public housing projects, Detroit began to lose manufacturing companies. During the 1960s and 1970s Detroit lost an average of about 7,000 factory jobs per year as factories moved to distant suburbs, to Southern and Western cities, and to industrializing nations in Asia and Latin America. Many of the less-skilled blue-collar jobs that were lost were replaced by white-collar jobs in finance and information exchange, but these new jobs required substantially more formal education than that obtained by most inner-city residents in Detroit (or other cities). This mismatch between skills required and skills possessed resulted in soaring unemployment, especially among African American males without high school diplomas.[33]

Building public housing projects near the center of an African American population, as Detroit did in the Gratiot redevelopment project, contributes to the further concentration and isolation of poor African Americans. No one in these areas has the capital to open neighborhood stores, so the kind of commercial activities that typically support enclaves are lacking. Higher-status African Americans who could serve as role models are also missing. In addition, family and neighborhood life suffers in these high-density housing projects. Residents feel little identification with the projects, and neighborly behavior such as looking out for each others' children or each others' property declines. Just when there was the most pronounced need for neighborly help (because of the large number of single-parent families living in poverty), that help and support was not available. Crime, teenage pregnancy, welfare dependency, gangs, and other problems increased.[34]

social problems?

Once many of these problems reach a certain threshold, they are worsened by self-perpetuating processes. For example, among those not directly involved, each crime that occurs encourages a "psychic withdrawal" from community life. Vigilance declines, the possibility of collective action is reduced, and crime is likely to increase further. Similarly, once any resident fails to properly maintain a home or apartment, the unsightliness reduces the incentive of neighbors to invest time or money in the upkeep of their own places.[35] In the public housing projects, the capacity of residents to collectively pursue their interests has been so weakened that drug dealers and gangs have been able to impose reigns of terror over tenants.[36]

Danger so suffuses everyday ghetto life that it creates an oppressive climate of fear that, along with the poverty of the area, results in widespread institutional withdrawal. Hospitals and public health facilities minimize their community involvement or move out of the area; the police and courts are overwhelmed; public schools, libraries, and youth clubs lack facilities and limit their functions.[37] With no "public space" left, there is no enclave. People remain in such places not because of any attachment but only because they have nowhere else to go.

service problems

*no public space
no enclave*

NOTES

1. For further description of the contrast between the RenCen and East Detroit, see B. J. Widick, *Detroit: City of Race and Class Violence,* Detroit: Wayne State University Press, 1989; and Wolf Von Eckardt, "Renaissance and Risorgimento," in Wilma W. Henrickson (Ed.), *Detroit Perspectives,* Detroit: Wayne State University Press, 1991.
2. See Widick, op. cit.
3. Ze'ev Chaffets, *Devil's Night,* New York: Random House, 1990.
4. Jerry Herron, *AfterCulture,* Detroit: Wayne State University Press, 1993, p. 133.
5. Quoted in Widick, op. cit., p. 233.
6. David M. Katzman, *Before the Ghetto,* Urbana: University of Illinois Press, 1973.
7. For further details on both riots, see NAACP, *Anti-Negro Riots in the North 1863,* New York: Arno Press and The New York Times, 1969.
8. Katzman, op. cit.
9. Ibid.
10. Ibid.
11. Arnold Shaw, *Honkers and Shouters,* New York: Collier, 1978.
12. Michael E. Dyson, *Reflecting Black,* Minneapolis: University of Minnesota Press, 1993. See also Amy Binder, "Reflecting Racial Rhetoric," *American Sociological Review* 58, 1993.
13. Philip H. Enis, *The Seventh Stream,* Hanover, NH: University Press of America, 1992. The "man snatcher" was one of the historical figures that combined with legendary figures to produce widespread beliefs among African Americans that "white demons" were trying to capture, burn, or otherwise destroy their bodies. This theme persists in inner-city rumors such as those that the twenty-eight African American children murdered in Atlanta were victims of the F.B.I., who wanted their bodies for research; and the Church's Fried Chicken franchise is owned by the Klan, and they put something in the chicken to make African American men sterile. See Patricia A. Turner, *I Heard it Through the Grapevine,* Berkeley: University of California Press, 1993.
14. Katzman, op. cit.
15. E. Franklin Frazier, *The Negro Church in America,* New York: Schocken, 1974.
16. Hans A. Baer, *The Black Spiritual Movement,* Knoxville: University of Tennessee Press, 1984.
17. For a review of these studies, see Richard A. Davis, *The Black Family in a Changing Black Community,* New York: Garland, 1993.
18. Willard B. Gatewood, *Aristocrats of Color,* Bloomington: Indiana University Press, 1990.

19. Katzman, op. cit.
20. George F. Bragg, *History of the Afro-American Group of the Episcopal Church,* Baltimore: Church Advocate Press, 1922. Reprinted by Johnson Reprint Corporation, New York, 1968.
21. Gatewood, op. cit., p. 126.
22. Ibid.
23. Wyn Craig Wade, *The Fiery Cross,* New York: Touchstone Books, 1987.
24. Widick, op. cit., p. 28.
25. *Detroit Free Press,* September 13, 1925, quoted in Henrickson.
26. Betty S. Jenkins, "Sojourner Truth Housing Riots," in Ibid.
27. David L. Good, *Orvie: The Dictator of Dearborn,* Detroit: Wayne State University Press, 1989.
28. Joe T. Darden et al., *Detroit,* Philadelphia: Temple University Press, 1987.
29. Reynolds Farley and William H. Frey, "Changes in the Segregation of Whites from Blacks During the 1980s," *American Sociological Review* 59, 1994.
30. Douglas S. Massey and Nancy A. Denton, *American Apartheid,* Cambridge, MA: Harvard University Press, 1993.
31. Gerald D. Suttles, *The Man-Made City,* Chicago: University of Chicago Press, 1990.
32. Darden et al., op. cit.
33. John D. Kasarda, "City Jobs and Residents on a Collision Course," *Economic Development Quarterly* 4, 1990.
34. William J. Wilson, *The Truly Disadvantaged,* Chicago: University of Chicago Press, 1987. See also Norman Fainstein, "Race, Class and Segregation," *International Journal of Urban and Regional Research* 17, 1993.
35. Massey and Denton, op. cit.
36. Langley C. Keyes, *Strategies and Saints,* Washington, DC: The Urban Institute Press, 1992.
37. Loic J. D. Wacquant, "Dangerous Places," in William J. Wilson (Ed.), *Urban Poverty and Family Life in Chicago's Inner City,* New York: Oxford University Press, 1994.

5

Chinatown in San Francisco and Little Taipei in Suburban Los Angeles

O f all of the nation's Chinatowns, the best known is probably San Francisco's. It was erected on the ashes of the Chinese Quarter, which was destroyed by fire following a massive earthquake in 1906. Until its destruction, the Quarter was the original point of entry for Chinese immigrants going anywhere in the United States, and it currently remains home to about 30,000 Chinese Americans.

The core of Chinatown is an old seventeen-block area densely packed with apartment buildings and housing projects, banks, markets, schools, cultural associations, restaurants, and professional offices. Its residents and proprietors are overwhelmingly Chinese. They also tend to be elderly and relatively poor. To the north and west of the core is a "greater Chinatown," which is several times larger than the core. This is a newer and less-crowded area that contains a Chinese plurality, but its stores and residences are occupied by a mixed population. Farther to the west lie Nob Hill and Russian Hill, described in Chapter Two. Although neither area still houses an elite enclave, the mansions of the area stand in marked contrast to the small shops and apartments of Chinatown. To the south and east, the core of Chinatown abuts San Francisco's main financial district, whose sky-scrapers provide Chinatown with another dramatic boundary.

Surveys show that a large proportion of Chinatown's residents feel relatively dissatisfied with the community. They dislike its noise, its filth, and its crowding. Chinatown is several times more densely populated than the remainder of San Francisco, and the steady influx of tourists and shoppers makes it difficult even to walk down the streets. The human congestion is made worse by the fact that meat and fish markets leave

Center City San Francisco

their refuse on pedestrian thoroughfares when they close their stores at night. Buses and cars compete for insufficient space on narrow streets, and there is frequent gridlock.

The city adopted a master plan for Chinatown in 1987. It was designed to alleviate the problems while at the same time to promote the community as both a residential enclave and as a tourist site; but those two objectives are difficult to balance. Furthermore, there is little that can be done about crowded, narrow streets and walkways without dramatically altering historic Chinatown, and its preservation is another important goal of the master plan.[1]

In short, there is little reason to believe that the crowded, noisy conditions of San Francisco's Chinatown will markedly improve any time soon. So why do the residents stay? Many remain because they are old and poor and have nowhere else to go. One older man who left China for America as a teenager is typical of this group. He traveled from Seattle to Chicago to Indianapolis to San Francisco searching for work. "I go all around the country, like a hobo I am," he said and laughed. After a stroke, however, he became unable to take care of himself and moved into one of Chinatown's many senior centers. "I never thought of spending my life here," he said, motioning to his small room in the center. "I got bad luck."[2]

Other residents could, of course, leave Chinatown if they wished. What do they like about living there? Their answers focus on factors that are the advantages of *any* enclave. They like being close to the Chinese restaurants and shops where they can obtain the goods and services available nowhere else. They also like the proximity to their relatives and friends, and are comfortable living in a relatively homogeneous community. Older residents in particular are likely to explain their attraction to the neighborhood with such comments as "Since I don't speak English, it's better for me to live here," or "I want to be close with my people."[3] For younger residents of both the core and noncore areas, closeness to place of work is another important part of neighborhood satisfaction. Chinatown is, for them, a place of residence and of work.

ENCLAVE ECONOMIES

Throughout the United States, Chinese Americans have continued to find employment within their enclaves, especially in small firms owned by fellow Chinese Americans. Between 1980 and 1990, for example, Asian-owned firms increased by 87 percent, compared with 14 percent for all firms nationwide. Within the Asian American grouping, the largest number were owned by Chinese, followed by Koreans. The Chinese-owned firms averaged three employees each, the greatest average number of employees of any minority group of business owners.[4]

While it is clear that Chinatowns generally, and that of San Francisco specifically, continue to provide employment for many Chinese Americans, there is some argument as to how much the employees benefit from this arrangement. On the one hand, studies in San Francisco have shown that Chinese Americans who work outside of the enclave in Anglo-owned companies receive better wages, on average, even when the comparison holds constant such factors as the industrial sector, type of job, and the workers' educational levels.[5] Because many ethnic-enclave businesses are poorly capitalized and operate in highly competitive markets, in addition to paying low wages, they often demand much of their employees. This leads many immigrant Chinese workers to complain that "Chinese . . . boss treats you like a working machine . . . much stricter than American bosses."[6] However, the Chinese newcomers who lack educational background and English language skills may have few alternatives to long hours and low pay in enterprises owned by other Chinese Americans.

On the other hand, there are probably advantages to working in an enclave that are difficult to detect in a conventional analysis of wages. For instance, stores in the enclave may be willing to hire poorly prepared workers who would not be considered employable outside the enclave.

There may be less racial harassment. Employment in enclave firms may also offer a promise of eventual co-ownership, which would be rare in firms not owned by co-ethnics. Therefore, the Chinese who immigrate to America with technical skills and college degrees may be best off working outside of the enclave, while those with limited skills and training have no choice but to seek whatever employment they can get within it.

There is another large group of workers about whom we know relatively little. These are the illegal immigrants who work in "underground economies." In San Francisco, New York, and other cities with large Chinese populations, immigrants who lack working papers take jobs in Chinatown's factories, stores, and restaurants. They frequently work long hours under difficult conditions and receive less than the minimum wage, but are nevertheless not entirely dissatisfied. Even an "immigrant sweatshop" has some compensations when the boss is a co-ethnic. For example, the Chai Feng sewing factory in New York City is owned and supervised by Maggie Zheng. She pays her workers less than minimum wage but serves them tea. She makes them work from 9 A.M. until midnight, with one fifteen-minute lunch break; but she provides the rice and tea lunch and drives them home at night. "She uses child laborers, but she fusses over them, combing their ponytails . . . even hugging them."[7]

To circumvent record keeping, the owner-managers of enclave businesses often pay in cash, which means that the workers have no medical, retirement, or other benefits. The presence of the illegal immigrants also drives down the wages of all less-skilled workers in the enclave. For example, one man begged his boss, the owner of a dry-cleaning store in San Francisco's Chinatown, to put his entire salary on the books. He had been receiving one-half of his salary under the table so that the owner could pay less in mandatory contributions and taxes. However, with only one-half of his salary on the books, the employee could not qualify for a mortgage. His boss not only refused the request, he replaced the employee with an undocumented immigrant who made no such demands.[8]

THE CHINESE '49ERS

In order fully to understand the origins of San Francisco's Chinatown, it is best to begin with the California gold rush of 1849. It attracted people from around the country and from around the world. Facing widespread famine in China, thousands of Cantonese peasants risked dangerous trips across the ocean to get to San Francisco and then to the gold mines. Most traveled on a credit system: Merchant brokers paid their passage in return

力

for promise of repayment, with hefty interest, from their future earnings. Ticket in hand, they were packed into ships like "herrings in a box."[9] Some of the immigrants wound up settling close to the San Francisco wharf where they landed. In 1850, a stretch of five blocks along Sacramento Street was called "Tong Yen Gai" (Street of the Chinese people). Within ten years it had doubled in size, had become known as the Chinese Quarter, and served as a provisional stop for Chinese prospectors. It later served the same role for Chinese immigrant railroad laborers and agricultural workers.

history

The Chinese prospectors, like the German, Irish, and others, moved across California, Nevada, and other Western states as word of big strikes spread. Life in these mining towns was rough and tumble, without much recourse to law, especially for the Chinese. Their baggy pants, pigtails, and "strange" eating habits set them apart, and they were robbed, beaten, and murdered with impunity. State laws also discriminated against them. In California, for example, the state legislature passed a law that required only "nonwhites" (of which there were then sizable numbers of two types, Chinese and Mexicans) to pay a prohibitive tax for mining.

In the mining towns that boomed after the discovery of gold or silver, the Chinese population was usually highly segregated as a result of prejudice reinforced by local ordinances. In Virginia City, Nevada, for example, white citizens could have a Chinese residence or business removed from their neighborhood simply by petitioning the board of aldermen. In the center of Virginia City was a "bawdy district," composed of saloons; boardinghouses; and flimsy dwellings in which prostitutes worked in small cubicles containing a bed, a chair, and a basin. At the northern edge of the bawdy district were the small dwellings and mud streets of Virginia City's Chinatown. In 1875 it was home to 1,254 Chinese men and 84 Chinese women, 75 of whom were prostitutes. By 1880, only about 20 Chinese women, all prostitutes, and 600 Chinese men remained; the rest had moved on.[10]

Most of the small Chinatowns that formed in Western towns during the latter part of the nineteenth century gradually disappeared. Some simply became too small to sustain a distinctive Chinese way of life. To find suitable marriage partners for their children, Chinese parents were forced to look in larger Chinatowns, the net effect being a population redistribution favoring the already larger enclaves such as San Francisco's. In addition, the only work for many of the men, according to sociologist Rose Hum Lee, was "women's work, i.e., cooking, washing, and domestic service," and there tended to be more demand for these services in larger cities.[11]

THE VICE QUARTER

As the gold fever of 1849 gradually dissipated, many of the Chinese prospectors turned for employment to the railroads being completed across the West. Along with new Chinese immigrants to the United States, these Chinese men found jobs cooking and cleaning for the railroad laborers. However, by the 1870s, most of the work on the railroad was completed. Thousands of Chinese men then returned to their original U.S. destination, San Francisco. In the relative safety of the Chinese Quarter, they took whatever jobs they could find in small factories, laundries, and restaurants. The Chinese men, desperate for work, were regarded by whites as causing lower wages by their willingness to work cheaply, and in retribution they were harassed in the streets and the courts. In San Francisco during the last decades of the nineteenth century, "Anti-Coolie Clubs" formed in every ward of the city. A "Pole Ordinance" prohibited carrying vegetables and clothes on poles while walking on sidewalks; the Chinese were the only ones who used such poles, so the objective of the law was clear.[12] Chinese salesmen and others who dared to venture outside of the Chinese Quarter were regularly "found strung by their pigtails to lampposts."[13] So the enclave grew during the late nineteenth century because Chinese immigrants were not welcome, and did not feel safe, anywhere else. It is clear that the enclave did not grow because it was a physically attractive place. First-hand accounts of late-nineteenth-century Chinatown described it as comprising "rat-infested . . . narrow alleys and underground cellars and secret passages, more like a warren of burrowing animals than a human city. . . . And Chinatown was accounted vicious because it was the haunt of gambling . . . and prostitution."[14]

Prostitution was historically associated with most Chinatowns because of the scarcity of Chinese women in America until after World War II. Almost all of the early Chinese immigrants were men traveling alone who intended to make their fortunes, then return to China and their wives or parents or both. In conformance with Chinese tradition, wives remained with their husbands' families, and in 1884 the U.S. Congress ruled that the Chinese Exclusion Act of 1882 prohibited the wives and families of Chinese laborers from entering the country. This act remained in effect until 1943.

At the turn of the twentieth century, there were hundreds of Chinese males for every Chinese female in the United States. Among all of the immigrants coming to America at this time there was a surplus of males to females, but the ratio was not nearly as lopsided among other nationalities as it was among the Chinese. The solitary Chinese males had limited heterosexual alternatives. Intimate relations with white women were hardly possible given the low standing of the Chinese. Marriages between whites and Chinese were prohibited by miscegenation laws in many states. Even white prostitutes were generally unwilling to engage in sexual relations with Chinese men. The answer was brothels staffed with young Chinese girls who were kidnapped from their villages in China; tricked into coming to California, ostensibly for an arranged marriage; or sold into slavery by destitute parents.[15] Those who could provide women made enormous profits. A woman who was sold for $400 in Hong Kong in 1880 was worth $1,800 in gold in San Francisco.

Gambling of various sorts has a long tradition in Chinese culture, so the appearance of faro, fan-tan, and other games of chance in Chinatowns is hardly surprising. The immigrant workmen who did not have families to go home to were looking for recreation within the enclave, creating a demand for places to gamble as well as for prostitution. Estimates are that around 1885, San Francisco's Chinatown had about 70 brothels, 150 gambling establishments, and an unknown number of opium dens.[16] The clientele was mixed, consisting of enclave residents, Chinese from the hinterlands, and some non-Chinese.

The "vice resorts" operated under the authorization (and with the protection of) criminal syndicates called "tongs." In 1900, there were an estimated thirty tongs in San Francisco's Chinatown, each of which claimed a monopoly on the brothels, gambling joints, and opium dens in its territory. These illegal activities persisted as a result of police complicity and the strength of the tongs, which rivaled that of any mafia, anywhere. The tong gunmen effectively protected member businesses and killed witnesses who might be a threat to their activities. The reach of the tongs was also extensive. The prostitution in Virginia City's Chinatown, for example, was controlled by tongs in San Francisco's Chinatown.[17]

Intermittent periods of peace and war characterized relations among San Francisco's tongs until the great earthquake and subsequent fire of 1906 destroyed most of the Chinese Quarter. The fire swept through the flimsily built enclave, scattering the residents. "Out of the narrow alleyways and streets they swarmed. . . . With bundles swung on poles across their shoulders, they retreated. . . . Smoke rose thousands of feet in the air."[18] The brothels and the opium and gambling dens that were the core of the tongs' operations were wiped out along with everything else. During the ensuing discussions of whether to rebuild the Chinese Quarter and where to put it, most of the tong leadership in San Francisco either retired or moved to other Chinatowns. The tongs never reorganized as a potent force in San Francisco's Chinatown, even though occasional rumors of tong killings and kidnappings continued. Tongs in New York, in contrast, are still associated with criminal gangs. The tong officials tend to be businessmen who own restaurants, travel agencies, groceries, and the like in New York's Chinatown, and double as the leaders of gangs involved in such activities as smuggling illegal aliens, murder, extortion, and prostitution.[19]

THE NEW ENCLAVE

The contemporary Chinatown in San Francisco was rebuilt a few years after the fire, on top of the site where the old quarter had lain in smoking rubble. It continued to attract newly arriving Chinese immigrants and other Chinese who had initially settled elsewhere in the United States. Essentially the same forces that had led to the growth of the earlier Chinese Quarter now led to the development of Chinatown. It again became a bustling and crowded residential and commercial area. However, China-town never again contained a proliferation of vice resorts like the old quar-ter, because of a number of social changes that were occurring during the early twentieth century. There was, as noted, the disassembling of the tongs that had organized vice in the prefire Quarter. In addition, opium use in the United States was down dramatically, discouraging anyone from rebuilding opium dens. Finally, as a result of high birth rates and a decline in male-predominated immigration, the ratio of women to men began to approach parity, leading to a decline in the demand for prostitutes.

The Chinese responded to these changes by replacing brothels and gambling dens with restaurants and nightclubs. The success of the Chinese in making this transition, where other groups had failed, was the result of their ability to make middle-class tourists feel secure in their enclave. Most nightclubs and restaurants, in order to be successful, must cater to middle-class couples. Attracting this clientele requires a higher level of security in the streets than attracting single men to a red-light district. Making the streets reasonably safe requires the kind of community organization that was present in Chinatown. The initial effort was also aided, sociologist Ivan Light notes, by the relatively small number of adolescent males who were then in the community. (It is adolescent males who are most likely to com-mit street crimes.) It was easier for the well-organized Chinese to control the small number of youths who had the highest potential of committing robberies and muggings. By keeping the streets safe, Chinatown's business sector successfully converted to a general tourist base.[20]

Ironically, the low status of the Chinese may also have been an asset in the growth of Chinese restaurants—restaurants being the heart of any tourist trade. Sociologists Gaye Tuchman and Henry Levine argue that Jews, and to a lesser extent Italians, were the most avid patrons of Chinese restaurants. Even though most groups favored the restaurants of their co-ethnics and worried about acceptance in the restaurants of other ethnic groups, everyone could "eat Chinese." There was no need to fear that one was overstepping some boundary, because the status of the Chinese was so low that no one felt threatened in their establishments. Customers could even make derogatory racial comments about Chinese waiters, and they would accept the insults without comment.[21]

Like any enclave, contemporary Chinatown is a product of the immigrants who first populated it. The Chinese immigrants who got off the boat on San Francisco's wharf and settled in nearby Chinatown were generally very poor. They came to the United States to seek wealth, but they had few skills to sell. When they arrived they also faced tremendous overt discrimination, which was backed up by government actions. They were pushed and pulled into a poor and crowded enclave, which has over the years retained many of the characteristics of its early residents.

THE LOS ANGELES CONNECTION

The Chinese immigrants of the last half of the twentieth century were very different from their earlier counterparts. Between 1949 (when the Communist Party took control of mainland China) and 1964 there were only about 70,000 Chinese immigrants to the United States. Some were political refugees, who tended to come from the well-educated professional and business elite. Others, who were equally well trained, came in pursuit of professional and technical positions, of which more were available in the United States than in China. After the liberalization in U.S. immigration policy in 1965, there was a dramatic increase in the number of Chinese immigrants: More than 850,000 entered the United States between 1965 and 1990. Many of them came with money and technical and business skills, standing in marked contrast to their nineteenth-century counterparts. Some moved to traditional Chinatowns such as the ones in San Francisco or New York, but the Los Angeles area has been the favored destination of the most recent Chinese immigrants.[22]

The current popularity of Los Angeles as a destination for Chinese immigrants is a result of changes in the world system as well as changes in the nature of the immigrants. Most nations have increasingly become part of a global economy in which major decisions are made in "world" or "global" cities. These are cities that house the headquarters of multinational corporations; are centers of finance, investment, and high-level legal and accounting services; and are major links in global transportation and communication networks. The institutions housed within these large and complex cities control and coordinate all kinds of business activities around the world. New York has historically been the preeminent world city in the United States and the nation's principal link to other world cities such as London, Paris, and Tokyo.[23]

As the United States has become more closely tied to the world system, more American cities have joined New York as important links in the international network. Los Angeles is of particular importance in this regard. Los Angeles' role as a world city has been enhanced both by the economic development of the Pacific Rim nations and by their internal political problems. During the 1970s, as relations between the United States and the People's Republic of China (PRC) were normalized, many wealthy families in Taiwan feared that their country would be reclaimed by the PRC. This fear prompted a capital outflow from Taiwan to the United States, with the Los Angeles area the favored destination of both capital and immigrants. By 1992, a total of twenty-two Chinese-owned banks had opened in the Los Angeles area; there were four nonstop flights daily from Los Angeles to Taipei (Taiwan's capital city); and greater Los Angeles had become the U.S. metropolitan area with the largest concentration of Chinese-owned firms.[24] Taking part in this exodus out of Taiwan were Mai Lin and her family. Mai Lin was 10 years old, in 1977, when her parents told her they were going to go to America. To California. To Disneyland. Her friends were all excited for her because everyone in Taiwan knew about Disneyland.[25]

The most recent Taiwanese immigrants in Los Angeles, as previously noted, have been very different from the earliest Chinese immigrants in San Francisco. Many had been professionals and executives in Taiwan and had access to substantial capital. Their transitions to lives in America, at least economically, were not difficult. In many less visible cases, however, immigrants made major life-style sacrifices in order to escape the communist threat, to offer their children a chance for a better life, or both. Mai Lin's parents left professional jobs in Taipei when the family got on the plane for Disneyland. He was a newspaper editor, she was a head nurse in a hospital. They could not duplicate their jobs in the United States. Mai Lin's father worked nights as a janitor, her mother as a waitress in a Chinese restaurant. The blow to his pride temporarily changed Mai Lin's father completely, causing him to become withdrawn and depressed. The parents' lives improved some years later, however, when they were able to buy a small franchise convenience store.

Despite many differences between the earlier and contemporary Chinese immigrants, both were like many other migrants in that large numbers of each group were attracted to a particular enclave, and that enclave grew with successive immigration. Many of the communities that have recently attracted the greatest numbers of Chinese immigrants are located in east suburban Los Angeles.

MONTEREY PARK: LITTLE TAIPEI

The first groups of Taiwanese immigrants to arrive in the early 1970s established an enclave in Monterey Park, a suburban area east of Los Angeles that is now known as "Little Taipei" to all of its residents. In the early 1970s, Monterey Park was a mostly white residential suburb, with Mexican

American, African American, and Japanese American minorities. During the 1980s, Monterey Park was actively promoted by realtors and developers in Taiwan, who sold it as "the Chinese Beverly Hills." By 1990 the majority of its population of 62,000 was Asian, with Taiwanese predominating. And the city was visibly Chinese, with Chinese ownership of most of the city's banks, supermarkets, restaurants, and newspapers.

The main commercial thoroughfare of Monterey Park is Atlantic Boulevard. On both sides of the boulevard are retail stores and commercial offices with large, colorful Chinese-language signs. Just east of Atlantic Boulevard, in the city's original downtown area, Garvey Avenue is lined with such Chinese businesses as restaurants, bookstores, herb shops, and banks, all with signs in Chinese. Even though journalist Timothy Fong was accustomed to seeing Chinese-language signs from visiting his grandparents in San Francisco's Chinatown, his first trip down Atlantic Boulevard nevertheless made his jaw drop. "It really did feel like a foreign country," he remembers thinking.[26]

Prior to the influx of immigrants that began in the 1970s, Monterey Park was a sleepy, tree-lined bedroom community of modest, single-family homes. That quickly changed when the Chinese refugees arrived. Using the capital they brought from China or could get from Chinese banks in Los Angeles, they began to build malls and condominiums and develop commercial strips. They converted the quiet downtown area into a busy commercial center. They took over many businesses, most of the restaurants, and all but two of the supermarket chains serving Monterey Park. "Bok Choy is more common than lettuce in produce departments, and dim sum . . . more readily available than a hamburger . . . in the restaurants."[27] Long-term, non-Chinese residents had a feeling of being overwhelmed by a foreign invasion.

One elderly white man complained, "Before, immigrants . . . lived in their own neighborhoods and moved into ours after they learned English. . . . Today, the Chinese come right in with their money and their ways. We are the aliens."[28] Another white man sold his home to a Chinese developer because he was disgusted with the changes that had occurred in his neighborhood. When he had moved into the house, the neighborhood had consisted of other individual family homes like his own. Now there were large condominium complexes on both sides of the street, filled with large Chinese families living in cramped quarters and speaking little English. "What I might do," he said, "is hang a little American flag on my truck and drive through town on my way out and wave goodbye to all my old friends."[29]

This feeling of being inundated by immigrants is, of course, not unique to the contemporary "natives" of suburban Los Angeles. At the turn of the twentieth century, Americans with Western European roots were expressing similar reactions to the Eastern and Southern European immigrants. To illustrate, the *Literary Digest*—an amalgam of newspaper and magazine stories from around the country—printed in 1900, "The swelling tide of immigrants from Southern Europe . . . who can not even speak our (language) . . . is a startling national menace that cannot be disregarded with safety."[30]

During the 1980s, the rapid influx of the Chinese into Monterey Park and the subsequent proliferation of commercial and residential construction changed forever the character of Monterey Park and caused traffic on its now-crowded streets to grind to a halt. The long-term residents of the city objected to the uncontrolled growth, as well as to the feeling of being invaded, and sought to resist further growth and immigration. The city council, dominated by whites, approved a master plan that greatly restricted further commercial development. (Similar growth-control issues have in recent years politically polarized a number of California communities.) Local governments do not generally tend to favor no-growth positions because continued growth, fueled by land development, enhances the fiscal situation of a local government.[31] Nevertheless, the no-growth policy was endorsed by Monterey Park's white-dominated city council, its intent rather clearly to inhibit further in-migration of the Chinese.

In addition, and if there was any doubt about the intent of the no-growth policy, English was declared the official language of Monterey Park. The council member who offered the most xenophobic regulations also tried to promote traditional symbols of patriotism and Anglo domination. In the spring of 1989, for example, he organized street parties in preparation for later fourth of July celebrations, and planned to speak at the one in his neighborhood. He never showed up, but what happened at the May picnic may offer a fascinating glimpse of a multicultural future. The largest group in attendance were elderly Chinese. They sat under a tree on which they had placed a banner with Chinese characters. The main speakers were Latino, and they wished everyone a "happy Cinco de Mayo." One speaker made a point of noting that the Chinese Lion dancers had been invited to perform at the main Cinco de Mayo event.[32]

The council member who had organized the neighborhood parties was voted out of office in 1990, receiving the fewest votes among the candidates from Anglos as well as from Chinese and Latino voters. The mayoral election was won by Judy Chu, an American-born woman of Chinese descent. As a former council member, she had spoken at length about separating ethnicity and xenophobia from growth policies. Her platform promised growth, but of a managed sort, and cultural diversity. It is difficult to tell at this time whether her election is a precursor of a new multiculturalism or just the result of a new balance of power. In either case, politics in the region is likely to be quite different in the future as Asians continue to spread out from "Little Taipei" across areas east of Los Angeles.

It should be noted that in other suburban areas east of Los Angeles, other Asian groups have formed enclaves that resemble Little Taipei in many respects. In Westminster, California, for example, a mostly Vietnamese population has established a community now known locally as "Little Saigon." Nearly 200,000 Vietnamese live in the area around Westminster and are served by the enclave's malls, modern shops, a TV station, and a radio station. It is the largest Vietnamese population in the world outside of Vietnam. Many of the Vietnamese who live here left professional positions and emigrated for political reasons. They opened banks, restaurants, and other shops that primarily serve the Vietnamese community. They even established a Vietnamese Chamber of Commerce. Like Little Taipei, many businesses in Little Saigon provide a connection between the enclave and the homeland; for example, one travel agent, who specializes in travel between Los Angeles and Vietnam, plans to build a retirement community in Vietnam for elderly people wanting to return to their native country.[33]

ASIAN AMERICAN WOMEN

Judy Chu's election as mayor of Monterey Park in 1990 was dramatic in terms of the way it demonstrates not only the shift in power to members of an ethnic enclave, but also the recent changes in the gender roles of Chinese women. Picture her inauguration in front of a packed room: well-dressed Chinese men recording the event on camera, large baskets of flowers with messages of good luck in red ribbons from Chinese individuals and associations, a gyrating Chinese dragon entertaining council members and visitors.[34] One hundred years earlier, Chinese women were bought and sold on San Francisco's wharfs. A potentially good prostitute was worth up to $3,000; a domestic slave unsuitable for brothel work could be bought for as little as $100. A few high-status Chinese prostitutes wore silk and jewels, but most dressed in plain cotton and charged 25 cents per customer. Their only escape from prostitution or slavery was suicide.[35]

Relatively few Chinese women, as noted, came to the United States until after World War II. Many of those who did come earlier came only as a result of being tricked or stolen as youngsters. Because of our interest in the establishment of urban enclaves in this country, we have focused primarily on the migrating males rather than the women they left behind. However, it should be apparent that the women who remained in China were part of the decision-making process. Migration decisions are almost always made at the household level, even when it is primarily men who, at least initially, migrate.

It would be easy to overlook the women's contribution to the economic position of their households after the women arrived in this country if one looked solely at their wages for labor outside the home. The Chinese (and other immigrant) woman plays a central role in maintaining the kinship and friendship ties that connect her household to the ethnic enclave. The various types of informational and economic assistance that co-ethnics offer each other, from housing to jobs, may be provided to members of one family from another because of kinship and social ties among their women.[36]

As Chinese women adjusted to life in America, they slowly encountered a somewhat different set of gender arrangements. Although women did not and have not reached economic parity with men in the United States, Chinese American women have had more opportunity to participate in the labor force than they had in China, and their relative status has been enhanced by their ability to contribute very directly to household income.[37]

For the women who were raised in the United States, learning how to combine ethnicity and gender in a meaningful way was often stressful. Mai Lin—who was introduced earlier as a 10-year-old leaving Taiwan for Disneyland—felt that her adolescence was especially difficult. Looking back at the time she was a senior in college, she felt that her adolescence was not just a matter of growing up and choosing what was right and wrong, but of choosing what was right and wrong in *each* culture. Chinese women are supposed to be submissive, she noted. And although she considers her life-style totally American, she also recognizes that she has internalized many Chinese values. So she tries to reconcile the Chinese image of women with an American image in which, it seems to her, women are supposed to be blond, blue-eyed, and fair skinned. Growing up was a difficult struggle because neither of the cultural images seemed to fit her very well.[38] (As a postscript, Mai Lin (a pseudonym) graduated with a degree in engineering from M.I.T. in 1989.)

Following the civil rights movement of the 1960s, Chinese women and men strove to improve the conditions of everyone in their ethnic group. Over time, this effort came to include all Asian Americans, rather than just Chinese Americans. This was partly because the differences among Chinese, Koreans, Japanese, and other Asians were starting to blur in response to the tendency of white Americans to include all Asians in a single category. A wider ethnic alliance also provided Asian Americans with more leverage in confronting a system, dominated by whites, that discriminated against all who were "other." Some of the initial efforts to improve Asian American women's roles resulted in the formation of women's caucuses within existing Asian church, civic, and professional associations. However, these groups tended to be male dominated and supportive of the status quo with respect to gender. Adherence to the traditional hierarchies of authority put Asian women in a particularly subordinate position to men.[39]

Feminist organizations dominated by whites had broader agendas that only partly met the needs of Asian women, so as Asian women became more aware of their multiply disadvantaged position—as females and as racial minorities—they established a number of Asian women's organizations. For example, in cities with large numbers of recent Asian women immigrants, Asian women's centers have been formed specifically to assist Asian women who are victims of domestic violence. Immigration-related stress, caused by loss of status or constant encounters with strange customs, seems to be a common precursor to domestic violence. The young Asian wife, traditionally subordinate to both her husband and his family, has been a favorite target for abuse in new and stressful settings. These centers have recorded numerous stories of women who have been punched and kicked by husbands and in-laws, sexually attacked, and locked in their rooms indefinitely. Lack of fluency in English and fear of officials in a strange society inhibit many from seeking help. To make matters worse, among South Asians the woman has traditionally been viewed as the guardian of family honor. If she sought outside help for domestic violence, she would be bringing shame on her family.[40]

The first problem faced by a woman whose situation is so bad that she is ready to seek outside help is to know who to call. In large cities, immigrant women's assistance programs have become highly specialized. In New York, for example, the Asian Women's Center operates a telephone help line, called "Sakhi," that specifically targets Indian women. The name means "a woman's friend" in Hindi, Urdu, and Bengali, and a friend is exactly what some of these women desperately need. One woman, after being married in New Delhi, moved to New York with her husband and his family. The husband proceeded to regularly kick her and pull her hair, sometimes in front of his parents. She eventually ran away and contacted Sakhi. "They really understood," she said, adding that "their being Indian really helped."[41]

Banding together has led many Asian American women to develop a feminist consciousness that helped them to overcome feelings of inadequacy and adjust to a new society. Most importantly, perhaps, they have learned that they can control outcomes in their lives.[42] As they have acquired more positive and more efficacious self-concepts, they have made possible such accomplishments as those of Mayor Judy Chu of Monterey Park.

NOTES

1. Chalsa M. Loo, *Chinatown*, New York: Praeger, 1991.
2. June Namias, *First Generation*, Urbana: University of Illinois Press, 1992, pp. 64, 65.
3. Loo, op. cit., pp. 81, 82.
4. Alexandro Portes and Min Zhou, "Gaining the Upper Hand," *Ethnic and Racial Studies* 15, 1992.
5. Suzanne Model, "The Ethnic Economy," *Sociological Quarterly* 33, 1992.
6. Victor Nee, Jimy M. Sanders, and Scott Sernau, "Job Transitions in an Immigrant Metropolis," *American Sociological Review* 59, 1994, p. 857.
7. *The New York Times*, March 12, 1995, p. 40.
8. For further examples from the Chinese and other immigrant enclaves, see *The New York Times*, June 13, 1993, p. 42.
9. Loo, op. cit., p. 32.
10. Marion S. Goldman, *Gold Diggers and Silver Miners*, Ann Arbor: University of Michigan Press, 1981.
11. Rose Hum Lee, "The Decline of Chinatowns in the United States," *American Journal of Sociology* 54, 1949, p. 425.
12. Loo, op. cit. For further details, see Roger Daniels, *Asian American*, Seattle: University of Washington Press, 1988.
13. Pardee Lower, *Father and Glorious Descendant*, Boston: Little, Brown, 1943, p. 9.
14. Albert W. Palmer, *Orientals in American Life*, New York: Friendship Press, 1934, p. 2.
15. Sanford M. Lyman, *Chinese Americans*, New York: Random House, 1974.

16. Daniels, op. cit., p. 22.
17. Goldman, op. cit.
18. Richard H. Dillon, *The Hatchet Men,* New York: Coward-McCann, Inc., 1962, p. 357.
19. See, for example, *The New York Times,* December 10, 1993, p. B3 and December 16, 1993, p. B9.
20. Ivan Light, "The Ethnic Vice Industry," *American Sociological Review* 42, 1977.
21. Gaye Tuchman and Henry G. Levine, "New York Jews and Chinese Food," *Journal of Contemporary Ethnography* 22, 1993. This pattern was strongly associated with New York, San Francisco, Chicago, and other cities.
22. Yen-Fen Tseng, "Beyond Chinatown: Chinese Ethnic Enterprises in Los Angeles," paper presented at the meetings of the American Sociological Association, August 1993.
23. Saskia Sassen, *The Global City,* Princeton, NJ: Princeton University Press, 1991.
24. Tseng, op. cit. See also Edward W. Soja, "International Restructuring and the Internationalization of the Los Angeles Region," in Michael P. Smith and Joe R. Feagin (Eds.), *The Capitalist City,* New York: Blackwell, 1987.
25. Namias, op. cit.
26. See the preface to Timothy P. Fong, *The First Suburban Chinatown,* Philadelphia: Temple University Press, 1994.
27. Ibid., p. 62.
28. John Horton, "The Politics of Diversity in Monterey Park, California," in Louise Lamphere (Ed.), *Structuring Diversity,* Chicago: University of Chicago Press, 1992, p. 223.
29. Quoted in Fong, op. cit. p. 65.
30. Quoted in Rita J. Simon and Susan H. Alexander, *The Ambivalent Welcome,* Westport, CT: Praeger, 1993, p. 93.
31. Stephanie S. Pincetl, "The Politics of Growth Control," *Urban Geography* 13, 1992.
32. Horton, op. cit.
33. *The New York Times,* February 12, 1993, p. 6.
34. Horton, op. cit., p. 217.
35. Goldman, op. cit.
36. Micaela di Leonardo, "The Female World of Cards and Holidays," *Signs* 12, 1987. For further elaboration of this position, see Nazli Kibria, "Vietnamese Refugee Success Stories," paper presented at the meetings of the American Sociological Association, August, 1993.
37. See the discussion in Silvia Pedraza, "Women and Migration," *Annual Review of Sociology* 17, 1991.

38. Namias, op. cit.
39. Esther Ngan-ling Chow, "The Social Construction of Asian American Feminism," paper presented at the meetings of the American Sociological Association, August 1993.
40. *The New York Times,* December 6, 1993, p. B3.
41. Ibid.
42. Esther Ngan-ling Chow, "The Development of Feminist Consciousness Among Asian American Women," *Gender and Society* 1, 1987.

enclave
- population identity
- geographic location
- economic conditions
- historical development
- culture (lifestyles, food, language
- institutions ⟮ church
    services ⟮ school
          ⟮ community center
        services

sociological concept.
social class
ethnicity / race
eth class
prejudice
discrimination
segregation
symbols

6

Miami's Little Havana

The center of Little Havana lies along 8th Street in Southwest Miami. It is one of several areas in Miami and its environs in which substantial numbers of Cuban Americans reside. As is typical in areas that served as initial enclaves for a particular group (Chinatown in San Francisco, for example) the current population of Little Havana is older and poorer than other, later, Cuban concentrations in the Miami area. Little Havana has retained a much larger population than other first enclaves such as Chinatown, however, and it continues to be the country's predominant Cuban American commercial and financial center.

Along 8th Street, for a stretch of several miles, are homes and apartments occupied primarily by Cuban families. Many of the homes have characteristically Cuban features such as decorative Spanish tiles, Catholic shrines in the backyards, and fences enclosing the front yards. There are many Cuban-owned stores, restaurants, and financial institutions catering largely, but not exclusively, to co-ethnics. Most of the stores were built before the Cubans arrived, and they are not architecturally distinguished in any way. The newer stores and shopping plazas do have Spanish elements in their facades, but it is their merchandise that is most distinctively Cuban. Some shops offer special wearing apparel such as guayaberas: lightweight, short coats traditionally worn by Cuban men. There are a number of botánicas selling religious goods, including potions for recalling saints and spirits and aerosol cans whose contents are guaranteed to improve one's love life. Many small grocery stores sell Cuban food products and almost all the pharmacies in Little Havana have signs in their windows announcing that they send medicine to Cuba. Local churches offer masses in Spanish and in English.[1]

A dozen or more daily and weekly Spanish-language newspapers are available at Little Havana's newsstands or from coin-operated boxes. Some of the newspapers are primarily oriented to news about Cuba and the Cuban population in the United States, whereas others focus on Latin America as a whole. The area is also served by WQBA, one of several Spanish-language

85

South Miami

radio stations, but the one that has historically claimed to be *La Cubanisma* (the most Cuban). Little Havana also contains a number of outdoor cafés and outdoor tables, where a mostly elderly male clientele gathers during the day and evening to play cards and dominos under black olive trees. A focal point in Little Havana is Domino Park, where older men play dominos throughout the day, smoke cigars, and talk about the old days in Cuba.

A number of Little Havana's restaurants offer traditional Cuban dishes such as chicken and yellow rice. Some of the restaurants are inconspicuous neighborhood eateries, others are highly ornate. The most famous among the latter is probably the Restaurant Versailles, "the mirrored palace," which was designed to closely resemble several once-popular night spots in Havana. Like its Cuban models, the Versailles has traditionally catered to a late-night crowd. Its mostly Cuban clientele is a mixture of party goers, loan sharks, politicians, and members of old Cuban society. This restaurant has been the scene of some legendary fights—both verbal and physical—between patrons involving disagreements over U.S. policies toward Castro and Cuba.[2]

SYMBOLIC ATTACHMENTS

Walking down Southwest 8th Street gives a former Cuban a feeling of being transported back in time to the Havana of yesterday. Little Havana in Miami is, in many respects, a copy of Havana in Cuba. Murals of the latter, complete with street signs, decorate the walls of restaurants, keeping alive memories of life in Cuba. As already noted, some of the establishments in Little Havana were even intentionally designed to mimic businesses in Havana. The nostalgia this creates, however, particularly for older residents, can be mixed with bitter irony. Havana of the 1950s was in many ways like a copy of Miami Beach with its overdone hotels and garish elegance. When Little Havana proceeded to imitate Havana, the former achieved "the unreal appearance of a copy of a copy."[3]

The paradox, according to writer David Rieff, is that it was easier to psychologically escape from Cuba in Cuba than in Miami! In Cuba, educated people were always eager to find out more about the rest of the world; for example, details about the latest European movies or American pop stars. In Miami, by contrast, it sometimes seems that Cubans only want to talk about Cuban films, Cuban music, and Cuban culture. There are, however, marked generational differences in Little Havana's residents' symbolic attachments to Cuba. Romanticized memories of all aspects of life in Cuba are most strongly held by the oldest cohort, which left in the 1960s. One Cuban American college student illustrated this tendency to romanticize by explaining how his Cuban mother always complained about the heat in Miami. It is a fact that the climate is very similar in Miami and Havana, but his mother insisted that it never got as hot in Cuba.[4] (Similar nostalgia for a romanticized vision of the homeland is also prevalent among many refugees from Southeast Asia.)

Among the older generation there is a shared nostalgia for their place of birth, and a yearning to return at least to visit. Havana has changed dramatically in the last generation, though. Cuban Americans are, as a result, left hoping to return to a place they would no longer recognize. To illustrate, after spending many years in Miami one woman returned to Cuba for a visit in 1991. She explained that even though she was born there, during her visit she felt like a foreigner. When she returned to Miami, she sadly realized there was nothing more for her in Havana. She had been "mourning for nothing all these years, and loving a place that no longer exists except inside us."[5]

The younger generation, on the other hand, is American born. Miami is home. While being of Cuban background is significant to them, many care more about the Miami Dolphins football team than about events in Cuba, and would rather eat at the local McDonald's than at the Restaurant Versailles. This does not mean that they have assimilated totally, though. A

1993 survey of eighth and ninth graders in a predominantly Cuban school in Miami is instructive. All of their parents migrated from Cuba. Almost all of these Cuban American youngsters say their knowledge of English is good, that they prefer English to Spanish, and that the United States is the best country in which to live. At the same time, most retain a strong identification with their parents' origins, referring to themselves as Cubans or Cuban Americans rather than simply as Americans, and 89 percent say their knowledge of Spanish is also good.[6] Thus for Cuban Americans in Miami a bilingual, bicultural life seems to be a reality, not just a possibility.

THE THREE WAVES

In order to understand the development of this distinctive community and the cleavages within it, Little Havana needs to be examined in relation to three waves of immigration.

FIRST WAVE $135,000$ wealthy

The first large movement of Cubans into Miami began in 1959. That was the year in which Fidel Castro's revolutionary army overthrew the Cuban dictator Batista. The Batista regime had promoted strong ties with the United States to facilitate the export of Cuban-grown sugar and the development of resort hotels and gambling casinos (staffed with local prostitutes) in Havana. To some Cubans, it seemed that Batista had turned Cuba into a colony and vice resort of the United States. Critics also regarded his regime as illegitimate because he became president as a result of a military coup. Castro's communist revolution promised to move the country away from its ties to the American business community and to redistribute wealth within Cuba. As one might expect, this message played better to the peasants than to the aristocracy.

Most of the Cubans who left between 1959 and 1961 (approximately 135,000 in all) considered themselves political exiles. They tended to be professionals, landowners, and industrialists who had seen their land and businesses confiscated by the revolution but were still able to take assets with them to the United States. They hoped Castro's regime would be short-lived, and they expected to be able to return soon to a post-Castro Cuba. Many of those who left Cuba at that time were already familiar with Miami from former visits. Located only ninety miles from Cuba, Miami's shopping centers and hotels had attracted both wealthy and middle-class tourists from Cuba throughout the 1950s. Miami offered an interesting combination of the familiar and the different to the exiled Cubans. The temperature, the palm trees, and even the architecture were largely the same in Miami and Havana.

For the Cuban tourists, it was exciting to see the familiar laid on a flat Florida landscape, surrounded by a different language.[7]

The failed Bay of Pigs invasion of Cuba in 1961 and the Cuban missile crisis of 1962 seriously strained relations between Cuba and the United States. Between 1962 and 1965 it was very difficult for Cubans to leave the island, and the average number of immigrants declined to about 25,000 per year. Most of those who left during these years were still people of means. Some were able to get their assets out of the country, but others came with little more than the clothes on their backs. For the latter, life in Miami held deprivations to which they were not accustomed. Rodolfo de Leon, for example, was 11 years old when his family left Cuba for Miami in late 1962. He remembers his life before the revolution, when his father owned several warehouses and his family lived in a large home. He also remembers Castro's victory and the soldiers and tanks driving down his street. Then, after his father's business was confiscated, his father tried to get passports quickly so the family could leave. They waited a long time in a suite in a fancy hotel, where Rodolfo recalls feeling like a millionaire. Then came a midnight telegram authorizing them to go, and all except his father (who temporarily stayed behind) left in a hurry.

Once in Miami, the family's Cuban pesos were not worth much. In helping to resettle the Cuban immigrants, the U.S. government provided all of them with food and financial assistance, but it supported only a meager life-style. Rodolfo remembers a whole year of eating canned meat and beans and fighting with his brother for the one pillow in their house. His mother eventually found unskilled work in a shrimp-packing plant, and when his father later arrived he picked tomatoes for 6 dollars a day.[8] Rodolfo's mother had never worked while the family lived in Cuba. She tended house, cooked, and watched over her children. In Miami, however, she had no choice but to work to support her family, even though being sheltered from the world outside the home was the traditional ideal for women in middle- and upper-class Cuban society.

Finding fewer barriers to paid employment for women in the United States, many immigrant women found themselves less economically dependent on men than they had been in Cuba (or other countries of origin). Under these conditions, traditional gender ideologies and patterns of social interaction usually change. Decision making, and social relations generally, tend to become more egalitarian.[9] For example, Rieff describes how one young Cuban American woman, a doctor, told her husband at a party that if she ever caught him with another woman she would shoot him. In *la Cuba de ayer* (the Cuba of old), well-born females did not talk that way. They were resigned to the probability that their husbands would be unfaithful. In Miami, at least the young Cuban American women learned to think differently, "to demand as well as to accept."[10]

SECOND WAVE *340,000*

An agreement between the United States and Cuba in 1965 allowed a program of "freedom flights," which brought a large second wave of 340,000 more refugees from Cuba between 1965 and 1973. Miami was their original destination, but it was the U.S. government's policy to try to induce Cubans who arrived during this period to leave Miami and settle throughout the nation. However, even among those relative few who did try life somewhere else, many returned. The Miami area has always been home to most Cuban Americans, and it continues to have a larger Cuban population and more Cuban businesses and institutions than any city in the world except Havana. As one Cuban American explained, "Miami is the only place in America where we Cubans can be ourselves."[11]

A great deal of insight into the adjustments Cubans had to make after arriving in Miami was provided by a series of surveys conducted by sociologists Alejandro Portes and Robert L. Bach. The investigators interviewed a representative sample of nearly 600 immigrants when they initially arrived in Miami in 1973. They then reinterviewed the respondents in 1976 and again in 1979. They were able to retain about 70 percent of the original members of their sample throughout the study, and the attrition that did occur did not seem to seriously alter the representativeness of the continuing sample.[12] They found that many in the Cuban community were in a state of flux during their first three years in Miami. Only about 25 percent remained at their first address, and about 25 percent moved more than once. During the second three-year interval, however, there was much more residential stability. About 50 percent stayed at the same address, and only about 10 percent moved more than once. By 1979, 40 percent owned their own homes. Occupational stability followed a similar pattern: In 1976 only about 8 percent of the Cubans who had arrived in 1973 owned their own businesses; by 1979, this figure had increased to 21 percent. Some became doctors or dentists; they tended to be young adults with wealthy parents, who could afford advanced education in the United States. Others, who also tended to have been wealthier before they left Cuba, established their own retail stores, repair service shops, and construction companies.

Many of the businesses begun in Little Havana were symbolically linked in the minds of the entrepreneurs to former businesses in Cuba. The tie is subtly, but dramatically, illustrated by the tendency of Little Havana businesses to note the date of their former establishment in Cuba as their official beginning. For example, the sign over the Caballero Funeral Home in Miami states, "since 1857." Miami did not yet exist in 1857, though, and the funeral home did not appear at this location until about 100 years after the advertised date.[13]

The growth of Cuban businesses was primarily dependent on the availability of start-up capital. Particularly during the 1970s, the international role of Miami's economy was growing, in some large measure due to the import–export and banking activities of the Cubans, which strengthened links between the economies of the United States and Latin America. A number of small Latin American banks were established in Miami. These banks were willing to invest in local businesses, and they hired as officials a number of local Cubans who had had extensive banking experience in Cuba. These banks provided start-up capital for Cuban entrepreneurs who could not have qualified for conventional loans at other Miami banks. Other capital was provided by many of the earliest refugees from Cuba, who had brought enormous assets to the United States; once it became apparent that they could not return to their former home, they too invested in local Cuban-owned businesses.

The steady stream of refugees also provided an abundant, and relatively inexpensive, supply of labor. They were hired by co-ethnics despite being unable to speak English and lacking American educational credentials. The readiness to hire relatively unqualified Cuban help was an expression of ethnic solidarity, though the workers' willingness to work cheaply was also an inducement to the Cuban owners. At the same time, even modest jobs in the enclave often provided an apprenticeship for those who wanted to learn how to operate an independent business. After gaining some experience the employees could borrow money relatively easily, start a business, and, in turn, hire later-arriving Cubans. Meanwhile, the continuous flow of Cuban immigrants also provided a sizeable number of customers for the goods and services that only enclave stores could provide.[14]

The status, on average, of the second wave of Cuban immigrants was lower than that of the Cubans who left when Castro first took power; but when compared to that of other immigrant groups throughout history, it was still relatively high. At the same time, Cuban immigrants in the second wave were diverse with respect to class, skin color, and ethnic background. "Cuban" and "American" did not exhaust the identities competing for salience, as the following two examples of second-wave immigrants illustrate:

> Antonio Wong was born in Cuba to Chinese parents. After they came to Miami, Antonio attended college in the United States, married, and bought a flower shop in Little Havana. He remembers the people in the Chinese community in Cuba experiencing open hostility. People made fun of the fact that they could not speak Spanish with a Cuban accent, but they still considered themselves Cuban and were frustrated by the unwillingness of other Cubans to accept them as such. Despite now being an

American citizen, Antonio feels that "inside" he is "still a Chinese wanting to be a Cuban." When his son is old enough, he hopes to take him to China. He has instructed the boy in Chinese religious and cultural traditions but has not told him about Cuba. The boy does not, in his father's view, need to know about it. "I am the one with Cuba inside. He will be another wandering Chinese who happens to like Cuban food."[15]

Isaac Cohen was a rabbi in Cuba who was raised in Havana. After emigrating to Miami he bought an electronics business. He became an active member of a Cuban Hebrew congregation, a Cuban Sephardic congregation (Jews who originally were forced out of Spain), and a Cuban Hebrew Circle. He refers to himself in summary as a "Jewban," which he defines as someone whose identity is very Jewish but who "also . . . speaks Spanish at home and eats Cuban food and dances to Cuban music."[16] He and his wife have deliberately taught their children to be Cuban, Jewish, and American. That way they will always have "two hyphens" in their self-concepts; and as a result of having two hyphens, he says, they will know with specific certainty who they are.

THIRD WAVE   125,000, lower class

Between 1973 and 1979 Cuba was virtually closed to any U.S. contacts. Cubans in Miami were largely unable to communicate with relatives in Cuba, while several hundred thousand Cubans who had applied for exit visas remained in Cuba under difficult circumstances. In 1980, thousands of Cubans wanting to enter the United States sought political asylum in the Peruvian embassy, and there were street demonstrations that embarrassed Castro. He invited Cubans in Miami to come to the port at Mariel and pick up their relatives. He announced that all were free to go.

During the next few months a poorly organized "freedom flotilla," financed by the Miami Cubans, eventually picked up 125,000 refugees at the port of Mariel. They were taken initially to the tip of Florida, Key West, then by bus to Miami. Five thousand were brought over during the first week alone, triggering alarm that the Miami Cuban community had opened Pandora's box and could not handle a refugee influx of this magnitude. Concern increased as descriptions of the refugees began to circulate.

The Cubans who were picked up at Mariel were a heterogeneous group. Some had relatives in the United States, some did not. The only uncontested characteristic of this third wave was that it contained a much larger lower-class contingent than had previous refugee groups. Castro vindictively claimed that the Mariel refugees were the "scum of the country," describing them as drug addicts, homosexuals, mental patients, and criminals. Later analyses of this third wave indicated that Castro exaggerated the "undesirable" aspects of the *Marielitos* in order to make the United States look foolish for accepting them. However, this third wave did contain both criminal and mentally ill contingents, and neither the Cubans in Miami nor the U.S. government knew exactly what to do with them.

The most negative view of the *Marielitos* was presented by the *Miami Herald*, the major daily newspaper in South Florida. It helped to crystallize negative feelings toward the newest refugees by reporting, at various times, that as many as 80 percent of the refugees came from Cuban prisons; that 20,000 were homosexuals; and that in the first three months after their arrival, local crime increased by 34 percent. The *Herald* also expressed the fear of the local Anglo business community that tourism in Miami and South Florida in general would be adversely affected by the presence of this large group of dangerous criminals.[17] Most of the media took a more benign view of the *Mariels*. For example, *Life* magazine in July 1980 published an editorial stating that while the newcomers did not represent the upper strata of Cuban society, the worst fears about their backgrounds were unfounded. A large part of the prison records of the refugees was attributed by the magazine to Cuba's tendency to punish its citizens for "buying scarce food on the black market or for speaking too openly against the government."[18]

The subsequent plights of the *Marielitos* in Miami were as varied as their backgrounds. Thousands were detained by U.S. government officials, who tried to return them to Cuba, but after extensive negotiations Castro eventually refused to take them back. They were subsequently held in federal detention centers, without due process, for a number of years. Psychiatric problems including depression and posttraumatic stress disorders were widespread among this group. What has been difficult to sort out is how much these problems were caused by their detention experience in the United States and how much they were a result of preexisting conditions. As many as 10,000 of the *Marielitos* may have been convicted of crimes committed in the United States. Again, however, it is difficult to know how much of the criminal behavior to attribute to adjustment stress, which may have been exacerbated by the tendency of the established Cubans to offer little help to the *Marielitos*.[19] At the other extreme, some of the refugees had close ties to established family in Miami and were readily integrated into the enclave.

The thousands of generally unskilled Cubans between the extremes described above sought whatever work they could find in Little Havana. The established Cuban community initially tried to shut out the *Marielitos*. Business owners in the enclave complained that the new refugees did not want to work, were shoplifters, and frequently became violent. The "native" white community, which had previously admired the Cubans' industriousness, responded negatively to the new image of the Cuban refugee. This negative image led to the passage in Dade County (which includes Miami) of an antibilingual referendum in the fall of 1980. The vote was received like a slap in the face by the Cuban Americans, who believed it was primarily directed at them. Until this time, the Cubans believed that they had been accepted by the mainstream of Miami, and this referendum was one of the events that led them to become a more self-conscious ethnic group.[20]

AFTER MARIEL

After the 1980 Mariel boat lift, the number of Cubans coming to the United States declined to an average of only a few hundred per year until 1988. When Soviet assistance to Cuba declined at that time, economic conditions on the island deteriorated, stimulating another increase in emigration. Between 1988 and 1993 immigration to the United States from Cuba increased to an average of about 3,500 per year. Illustrative of this group of refugees is the Gonzalez family: Pedro, who worked as an automobile mechanic; Maura; and their 12-year-old daughter. In 1992 as the Cuban economy was crumbling, Pedro bought a boat on the black market and kept it with a friend who lived near the port at Mariel. They bided their time for two years, until it appeared that Cuban officials would do little to stop them if they tried to leave. They left quickly, with little more than the clothes on their backs and ham sandwiches and Pepsi, also purchased on the black market. After two days at sea, the Coast Guard picked them up and brought them to Key West. From there they went to Little Havana to live with an aunt who had moved there a number of years earlier. They left Cuba expecting to improve themselves economically and to find a better life in Miami. "I want what I've never had before," Maura said. "We never celebrated Christmas in Cuba."[21]

During 1994 there was another surge in the number of Cubans taking to motorboats, rubber dinghies, and rafts in an effort to leave the island. They got caught up in international politics, however. The U.S. government unilaterally maintains an economic embargo on Cuba, which has been strongly supported by the Cuban community in Miami. When the Hemisphere Trade Talks opened in Miami in December 1994, nearly 100,000 Miami Cubans held a rally to express their support for continuation of the embargo. To pressure the United States to lift the embargo, the Cuban government periodically relaxes its surveillance, permitting thousands more Cubans to try to leave for Florida. The exodus that follows such a relaxation of Cuban exit policy enforcement overwhelms the ability of the United States to process the immigrants—exactly Castro's intent. Unfortunately, the

1994 refugees became pawns in the battle; they were placed in detention camps at the United States' Guantanamo Bay Naval Station in Cuba, with an overflow detained at the U.S. base in Panama. At the end of 1994, over 20,000 were being held at Guantanamo, over 8,000 in Panama; all were living under very difficult conditions.[22] Some of Miami's Cubans have responded by urging the United States to end the embargo, but they have continued to be overwhelmed by the opposition in their own community.

GENERATIONAL DIFFERENCES IN LITTLE HAVANA

The Cuban American population of the Miami area numbers nearly three-quarters of a million persons. Their views on Cuba are separated from each other by marked generational differences. As previously noted, the oldest immigrants are the most attached to Cuban ways of life, Cuban food, Cuban clothing, and so on. This oldest generation tends to favor a U.S. policy that continues to punish the Castro regime until he, and the rest of the communist leadership, are forced out of power. Many of the younger Cuban Americans, on the other hand, either do not share this hatred of Fidel Castro or they want to find a constructive way to be positively involved in Cuba's future despite their feelings toward Castro.

Because of the wealth and political power of the Cuban community in Miami, the Castro regime has periodically tried to win them over, but with limited success. From the Mariel boat lift in 1980 to 1994 there were no nonsurreptitious contacts between representatives of the exile community in Miami and the Castro administration. In the Spring of 1994, Cuba offered to ease restrictions on return visits, and this induced a group of about 200 Cuban Americans to fly to Havana for "official" talks. The Cuban government's objectives were to attract investments from the exile community and to persuade them to use their domestic political influence to end the U.S. embargo on exports to Cuba. However, little progress was made in the talks, primarily because so many older Cuban Americans continued to be unalterably opposed to any acts of reconciliation.

One of the Cuban American participants in the conference was Magda Montiel Davis. She was a prominent attorney in Little Havana and in 1992 was the (unsuccessful) Democratic candidate for U.S. Congress. As the talks in Havana ended, she said good-bye to Castro and thanked him, then reached over and lightly kissed his cheek. The kiss was caught on film, and was strongly denounced on Spanish-language television and radio stations in Miami. There was such an outpouring of angry threats that she was given police protection. Five of her employees publicly resigned in protest. They were immediately offered jobs in the private sector by wealthy businesspeople in Little Havana and jobs in government by the county commissioner, who is also a Cuban exile. Ms. Montiel was also pressured to resign from several Cuban American organizations. Her father, like most of his generation, has always been vehemently anti-Castro; according to family friends, her actions broke his heart.[23]

The complex generational differences in Little Havana are also illustrated by the tumult surrounding Carlos Varela, a popular Cuban singer. He has developed a large following among young people in Cuba and Miami but not among older people. Teenagers and young adults regard him as capturing the mood of "disgruntled youth." To older Cuban Americans in Miami he is still part of the Cuban system, even though Cuban officials have banned his videos. The older generation in Miami argues that his music is cynically used by the Castro regime to make outsiders think that dissent is possible there. After receiving his latest video, MTV deliberated for six weeks before airing it, out of concern that they would alienate members of Miami's affluent and powerful Cuban American enclave. It was in this delicate context that an employee of the Spanish-language network of MTV, headquartered in Miami, was privately helping to organize a concert tour in Havana by Mr. Varela. MTV Latino was not involved, but the employee used stationery with the company's logo in sending a fax. The Cuban American National Foundation, headquartered in Little Havana, called the station to protest. They claimed that travel to Cuba was "immoral" and violated American policy. Callers to the station threatened advertiser boycotts and bombings. The employee, an assistant to the managing director, was dismissed five days later. The letter of dismissal said that her actions had "placed the company at risk," although MTV Latino claimed it was because she used company resources for a personal matter.[24]

Cutting across the generational differences among Cuban Americans are the solidifying effects of a common heritage and language. Another major contributor to solidarity among Cuban Americans is conflict with outsiders. *Outsiders* sometimes includes the larger Anglo community, but the most intense conflicts have occurred between the Cuban American and African American communities in Miami.

CUBAN AND AFRICAN AMERICAN CONFLICT

There was tension between the Cuban American and African American communities during the 1960s and 1970s because of economic competition. In many cities, this was a period of economic progress for African Americans, which was associated with the civil rights movement. However, in Miami, African Americans felt that not only were they not making progress, they were losing ground in the private sector because of the Cuban refugees. The Cubans competed with African Americans for the same service jobs in such businesses as restaurants and hotels, the garment industry, and construction. A number of African American groups complained that African American workers were being pushed aside to make room for Cubans.[25] Then, Cuban-owned gasoline stations, groceries, and laundromats began springing up in African American neighborhoods, sometimes replacing African American–owned establishments. The Cuban enterprises were sometimes conspicuously more successful, as well. Analysis of business income by race indicated that, in fact, the average earnings of Cuban-owned enterprises were approximately twice those of the African American-owned businesses.[26]

African Americans also felt that Cubans were benefiting at their expense in the public sector. For example, during the 1960s and 1970s the U.S. government was providing Cuban refugees with relocation assistance, which, African Americans felt, might otherwise be used to assist people in African American neighborhoods, who had been systematically discriminated against in Miami for many years. During this period, Cuban-owned contracting companies also received several times more minority funding than African American–owned firms, both from Dade County and from the U.S. Small Business Administration.

The resentments of African Americans in Miami have on several occasions resulted in serious rioting. Of particular importance to the Cubans, who were feeling "picked on" during public discussions of Miami's antibilingual referendum, was a street demonstration in May of 1980. It occurred after an all-white jury acquitted four white police officers of having beaten a black insurance agent to death in Miami. It was at least the fifth racially divisive case in a fifteen-month period, which led most people in Miami's African American communities to believe that the criminal justice system did not treat them fairly. This latest decision became the immediate precursor to a particularly violent riot. Businesses, some of which were Cuban owned, were looted and burned. Nonblacks who were caught driving through the riot area were viciously beaten, and eight were killed. One victim, a Cuban-born butcher, was clubbed to death by a mob wielding sticks, who then set his body on fire. His wife and son were at that moment waiting at the Mariel harbor for a boat to take them to Miami.[27] The riot of 1980 was not primarily directed at Cubans, but combined with more symbolic rejections by the Anglo community, it contributed to the Cuban community's cohesiveness.

In order to fully understand the continuing conflict between Cuban and African Americans in Miami, a third group—the Haitians—must also be taken into account. In 1980, simultaneous to the Mariel flotilla, thousands of Haitian "boat people" were trying to escape persecution or miserable living conditions and enter the United States. Coast Guard cutters attempted to block their way, and immigration officials either deported or jailed most of those who got through. Such magazines as *The Nation* described the treatment of the Haitian boat people as "disgraceful" and "punitive and vindictive."[28] Jesse Jackson, Andrew Young, and other leaders of the African American community saw color as the issue. The Haitians were, of course, black. Was that why they were turned away while the Cubans were admitted? Following African American–organized marches in Miami and elsewhere, some Haitians were eventually admitted. They congregated on Miami's northwest side, in an area that came to be called "Little Haiti." It was a poor community comprising young people living in stucco cottages. Little Haiti encroached on previously established African American (not Cuban) communities, and the Haitians proceeded to compete with African Americans for the low-skill jobs not taken first by Cubans. However, despite the competition, Miami's African Americans continued to support Haitian immigration and relocation assistance, arguing that Haitians should receive the same preferential treatment as Cubans. In the local Cuban community this was seen as anti-Cuban.

Many of the Haitians hoped to emulate the entrepreneurial success of the Cubans, but they lacked comparable economic resources, and the U.S. government's treatment of the Haitians was also much less supportive. Little Haiti bears no resemblance to Little Havana. The experience of Haitians in Miami has in fact been much closer to that of people in poor African American communities. The previously described survey of eighth and ninth graders in Miami schools is instructive here. The black Haitian children, when asked whether they had ever experienced discrimination, often responded with "this loud 'Pssh!' Like, 'what a stupid question.'" Two-thirds of them said that they did. In contrast, discrimination was so alien to many of the Cuban youngsters that some did not even understand the question. Only 29 percent said that they had ever experienced discrimination.[30]

In addition to the issues surrounding Haitian immigration, the positions of Miami's African American and Cuban communities have dramatically diverged on other matters that have resulted in conflict. When South Africa's Nelson Mandela was invited to speak at a convention in Miami in 1990, for example, African American leaders were enthusiastic. As part of his tour, high elected officials had already greeted him warmly in Washington, New York, and elsewhere. The African American community felt that Miami should do the same. The Cubans, however, were opposed to according him VIP treatment because of the prior support he had expressed for the Castro regime. The Cuban position won, and Mandela's official welcome to the city was muted. When Mandela arrived to speak,

African American groups greeted him with such signs as "Welcome to Miami, Home of Apartheid."[31] A week after Mandela's visit, there were major street demonstrations in Miami as blacks (including Haitians and African Americans) protested the city's treatment of Mandela, which they blamed on the Cubans.

The Miami Cubans' intense interest in the implications of any government policy for Castro's regime, combined with the domestic conflicts described above, led to a determined effort in the Cuban community to become more powerful politically in Miami. They had the demographic base and the wealth. From headquarters in Little Havana, Cuban Americans energetically entered local and regional politics. In the 1980s and 1990s, Cuban Americans were elected or appointed to many key positions in Miami and its county, including mayor, city manager, and superintendent of schools. In many instances, African Americans were the defeated candidates, and this has contributed to continuing strain between the two groups. In December 1990 the *Miami News,* a black-oriented newspaper, on page one expressed the view of many African Americans when it headlined the charge, "Miami Run By Cuban Mafia."[32]

EXILES AND IMMIGRANTS

Theories of international migration have assumed that the motivation of the traditional migrating person or household is primarily economic. More jobs, better jobs, and better wages are anticipated in the country of destination than in the country of origin. The direction in which people move and the rate at which they move have therefore been explained by a world systems view that sees movement occurring in response to "disruptions" in the development of poorer countries. Specifically, in searching for cheap labor and materials and new consumer markets, firms in the capitalistic nations that dominate the world economy invest in the less-developed (frequently former colony) nations. As these investments transform the recipient communities, one result is a weaker attachment of natives to their local economies, which leads to a tendency for them to seek better opportunities elsewhere. They frequently move to major world cities—such as New York, Los Angeles, and Miami in the United States—where they typically take low-paying, low-status jobs with little possibility for upward mobility. As the stream of migration from one place to another continues, networks are established that facilitate further movement of co-ethnics into enclaves in world cities.[33]

The above description of the traditional immigrant fits some of the Cubans who moved to Miami, especially the *Marielitos.* It would also fit the nineteenth-century movement of Chinese, Italians, and Irish to America and such contemporary immigrants as Mexicans in various Texas cities. On the other hand, the traditional immigrant profile misses some important features of other groups such as the first wave of Cubans to settle in Miami or the recent immigrants from Taiwan who moved into the Los Angeles area. For the latter groups, avoiding political or religious persecution is a major motivation for moving, and these people are often referred to as exiles rather than immigrants.[34]

The distinction between traditional immigrants and exiles is associated, in general, with two sets of differences: (1) The age and sex distribution of exiles is more likely to be balanced; that is, they have the same demographic characteristics as the larger population of which they are a part. This balance is maintained because all family members are likely to leave simultaneously in order to avoid persecution. In contrast, selective migration, which characterizes most traditional immigrants, results in an underrepresentation of women and children; men come to seek their fortunes and their families follow later. (2) The occupational and income levels of exiles in their country of origin tends to be higher than that of traditional immigrants, but exiles frequently experience downward mobility, at least initially, in their country of destination. (When changes in the country of origin result in high rates of student immigration, however, this socioeconomic difference may disappear.)

The differences between traditional immigrants and exiles may result in some corresponding differences in the enclaves each group establishes. Immigrants have most often formed temporary communities, way stations on the path to greater assimilation. The immigrant groups generally lacked both the economic and the demographic supports necessary to develop enclaves that were truly self-contained and that offered sufficient prospects to keep young people from moving out. They could not retain their youth because most of their economic opportunities lay outside the enclave; so too did political power. The enclaves of exiles, on the other hand, have been able to offer their residents better economic opportunities. Exiles have also been able to wield more political power and to exert more control over the conditions under which their members live and their relations with other groups. As a result of these differences, the enclaves of exiles may prove to be more enduring than those of traditional immigrants.

Finally, we must note the tendency of exiles to regard themselves as being in a temporary situation; they are in exile only until some event occurs such as the death of a religious leader or the collapse of a political regime. Traditional immigrants are mixed in this respect. Some intend to accumulate money and return home, whereas others see their country of origin as unlikely ever to offer sufficient opportunities. Some traditional immigrants and some exiles do return, but they are the minority. Even among those exiles who always profess the desire to return, it is not certain that they really would, even under the conditions they specify. It is common for Cubans in Miami to solemnly toast each other with the phrase, "Next year in Havana," but they probably mean it mostly at a symbolic level. One self-defined exile told Rieff that he would try to get to Havana on the first available plane if Castro were out of the way. "Are you really sure?" Rieff asked him. "Well," he smiled, "Who can tell?"[35]

NOTES

1. Thomas D. Boswell and James R. Curtis, "The Hispanization of Metropolitan Miami," in Thomas D. Boswell (Ed.), *South Florida: The Winds of Change*, Miami: Association of American Geographers, 1991.
2. José Llanes, *Cuban Americans*, Cambridge, MA: Abt Books, 1982.
3. Ibid., p. 129.
4. David Rieff, *The Exile*, New York: Simon & Schuster, 1993.
5. Ibid., p. 204.
6. The figures given were reported in *The New York Times*, June 29, 1993, p. A10. All the Cuban American youngsters were enrolled in private Cuban American schools in Miami, so their answers may not be typical of all Cuban Americans of their age in Miami. Nevertheless, the results are highly suggestive.
7. Alejandro Portes and Alex Stepick, *City on the Edge*, Berkeley: University of California Press, 1993.
8. June Namias, *First Generation*, Urbana: University of Illinois Press, 1992.
9. For a general discussion of this issue, see Silvia Pedraza, "Women and Migration," *Annual Review of Sociology* 17, 1991.
10. Rieff, op. cit., p. 157.
11. Ibid., p. 156.
12. Alejandro Portes and Robert L. Bach, *Latin Journey*, Berkeley: University of California Press, 1985.
13. David Rieff, quoted in Portes and Stepick, op. cit.
14. Portes and Stepick, op. cit.
15. Llanes, op. cit., p. 104.
16. Ibid., p. 113.
17. Portes and Stepick, op. cit. The Cuban community's resulting displeasure with the *Herald* did not end with its coverage of the Mariel immigrants. There was a succession of news stories that gave Cuban Americans the feeling that the newspaper was not sympathetic to Cubans. In the late 1980s, the *Herald's* parent company established an editorially autonomous Spanish-language edition of the newspaper, primarily oriented to Miami's Cuban population. It is now published daily in Miami.

18. Rita J. Simon and Susan H. Alexander, *The Ambivalent Welcome,* Westport, CT: Praeger, 1993, p. 179.
19. For further discussion of stress and maladaptive behavior among the *Marielitos,* see Roberto J. Velasquez and Michaelanthony Brown-Cheatham, "Understanding the Plight of Cuba's Marielitos," in Ernest R. Myers (Ed.), *Challenges of a Changing America,* San Francisco: Austin & Winfield, 1994.
20. Portes and Stepick, op. cit.
21. *The New York Times,* August 19, 1994, p. A14.
22. For a description of the difficult lives of refugees in these camps, see *The New York Times,* December 10, 1994, p. 6.
23. *The New York Times,* May 6, 1994, p. A10.
24. *The New York Times,* June 9, 1994, p. A12.
25. Raymond A. Mohl, "On the Edge: Blacks and Hispanics in Metropolitan Miami," *Florida Historical Quarterly* 69, 1990.
26. Bruce Porter and Marvin Dunn, *The Miami Riot of 1980,* Lexington, MA: D.C. Heath, 1984.
27. Ibid.
28. Quoted in Simon and Alexander, op. cit.
29. Portes and Stepick, op. cit.
30. *The New York Times,* June 29, 1993.
31. Ibid., p. 176.
32. Quoted in Portes and Stepick, op. cit., p. 251.
33. For a discussion of this traditional view, see Douglas S. Massey, "Theories of International Migration," *Population and Development Review* 19, 1993.
34. See, for example, Georges Sabagh and Mehdi Bozorgmehr, "Are the Characteristics of Exiles Different from Immigrants?" *Sociology and Social Research* 71, 1987. This distinction between immigrant and exile can blur, however, when exile is self-imposed and motivated by the desire to maintain a high economic life-style that is threatened by political events.
35. Rieff, op. cit., p. 45.

7

Gays and Lesbians in San Francisco's Castro and Mission Districts

San Francisco is a city in which alternative life-styles flourish, often side by side. Of particular interest to us in this chapter are the gay and lesbian enclaves and subenclaves that have formed in the city. Similar concentrations are found in Los Angeles, New York, Boston, and elsewhere, but the largest and the institutionally and commercially most complete gay and lesbian enclaves are in San Francisco, and they will therefore be the primary focus of this chapter. To put these enclaves into a larger context, we begin with a brief overview of the city.

A SAN FRANCISCO OVERVIEW

At the northeast edge of the city a number of piers jut into San Francisco Bay. If a person started there and began walking toward the center of the city, North Beach would be reached in less than one mile. This area contains a number of bars, restaurants, and theaters, and, as in many other parts of San Francisco, the recreation and entertainment are oriented to diverse tastes. For example, set among "conventional" restaurants and bars is Finocchio's, a North Beach nightclub that features female impersonators and live music in three nightly shows. Continuing south and west, toward the center of the city, one brushes on the outskirts of Nob Hill (discussed in Chapter Two). At the edge of Nob Hill is a concentration of playhouses and theaters that host both traveling and local productions. There is also the Nob Hill Male Show Palace, which offers live male strippers onstage, plus private viewing booths, magazines, and novelties.

Just a few blocks farther south and west, the Tenderloin district begins. This once served as a transit point for sailors and was home to most of the city's prostitutes. In the 1950s it also contained most of the city's gay bars. It still contains a few, mostly catering to men who cross dress, or "drag queens." This fact earned it the nickname "Valley of the Queens" in local gay circles.[1] The Tenderloin also has an assortment of cheap bars and hotels that accommodate winos and bums. At the southern edge of the Tenderloin, Golden Gate, 6th and Market Streets converge. Market is the major thoroughfare in the central city. On the south side of Market, opposite the Tenderloin, is an area aptly called "South of Market." It was once a warehouse district, but the addition of a large number of bars, nightclubs, restaurants, and discotheques has turned South of Market into a center for nightlife. It attracts an extremely diverse clientele: people dressed in conventional business suits and others in outlandish outfits, young and old, gay and straight, laborers and professionals.

In San Francisco's gay community, the South of Market area is often referred to as "Valley of the Kings" (in contrast to the Valley of the Queens) because many of the gay-oriented bars, bookstores, and nightclubs have a highly masculine ("leatherman") emphasis. Commonplace dress includes motorcycle jackets and boots and studded wristbands. The names of many of the businesses in South of Market also convey this macho emphasis: The Stud Bar, The Arena Bar, and Folsom Gulch Adult Books, to name a few. Entertainment in the gay bars and nightclubs has also tended to be congruent with this theme. For example, one bar staged "slave auctions," in which a volunteer was stripped and tied by other men in black masks and the "slave" was sold for the night to the highest bidder.[2]

Continuing down Market, one passes a number of government office buildings, auditoriums, and the city's main library and then comes to 17th Street, where Market and Castro intersect. To the south, down Castro Street, is the Castro district. Located within the Castro are many stores, professional services, and institutions serving a gay clientele, and residential areas in which gays predominate. Unlike centers of nightlife, which may be strongly gay oriented but remain limited in scope, the Castro is an enclave in every sense of the term.

Just north of the Castro district is Haight–Ashbury. During the 1960s it was the center of the hippie community, which contained a number of gays and lesbians, and some of the Haight's bars became notable hangouts. A lesbian bar named Maude's, which opened in 1966 and closed in 1989, later inspired the documentary film "Last Call at Maude's."[3]

About one mile east of Castro Street, running parallel to it, is Valencia Street, in the Mission district. It is a center of retail stores and institutions, many of which serve a lesbian clientele, and there are lesbian residential concentrations in several surrounding neighborhoods. The area around Valencia Street has some of the qualities of an enclave, but, as we will later explain, it does not hold a lesbian majority and is not institutionally complete.

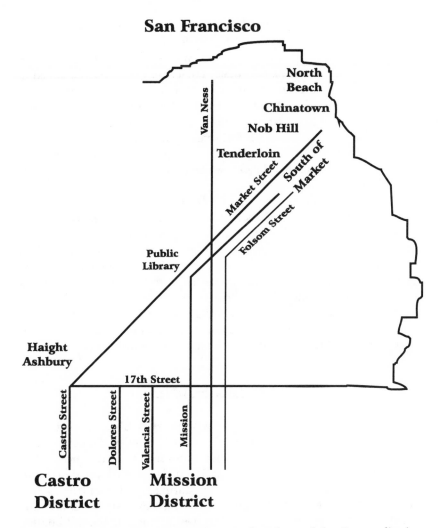

San Francisco

Although it may be best regarded as a subenclave of the Castro district, Valencia Street in the Mission district is the commercial and institutional center of the most fully developed lesbian community in the United States. In this respect it is analogous to Castro Street in the Castro district.

Most of this chapter will be devoted to a discussion of the gay and lesbian concentrations in the Castro and Mission districts of San Francisco, and to an analysis of the alliances and conflicts between them. Neither enclave began to take its contemporary form until after 1970, but if we want to understand how these enclaves emerged in the center of San Francisco and the meaning of these places to the groups who live in them, it will be helpful to begin with a look at some of the effects of World War II on American life.

During World War II, San Francisco was a major port for military personnel going to or coming from the Pacific. When homosexual service-people were periodically purged by the military from the Pacific theater, they were usually shipped back to San Francisco. Thousands remained in this city rather than return home in the disgrace of a dishonorable discharge. When the war ended, thousands of other homosexual ex-GIs also chose to remain in San Francisco rather than return home to small towns in the Midwest, where life as a homosexual now seemed impossible. Many homosexual veterans who did go home after the war soon returned to the less oppressive climate that they knew from their wartime experience they would find in San Francisco.[4]

The war is also credited by many with having created settings in which people were given opportunities to discover their homosexuality. Millions of young servicemen and women were living in same-sex quarters in the military, and millions of young civilian women were living in communities from which most of the young men were gone. For some people, the living arrangements imposed by the war merely reinforced previously established homosexual patterns. For others, however, same-sex living was conducive to experiences that led them to realize that they were sexually interested in people of the same sex.[5] With this discovery, many homosexuals sought out others who were like them, and San Francisco was a magnet to them.

THE BAR SCENE

During and after the war, concentrations of homosexuals supported a proliferation of bars primarily catering to gay and/or lesbian clienteles. These developments were most marked in port cities such as San Francisco, Los Angeles, Boston, and New York. Similar bars had been established earlier in a number of cities. In New York's Harlem during Prohibition (the 1920s), for example, middle-class gay and lesbian whites and African Americans mixed in small clubs that featured transvestite floor shows and bootleg liquor.[6] However, with the more concentrated markets that developed after World War II, it became economically feasible for bars to specialize. In fact, competition among bars spurred each to find its own niche by attracting a gay or lesbian clientele with distinctive interests and life-styles.

An interesting illustration of this specialization process is provided by the lesbian bars of Montreal. The first lesbian-only bar in the city opened in the 1960s. Called Baby Face Disco, it was owned by a tough-acting ("butch") lesbian known only as Baby Face, who was also the manager and bouncer. It had a jukebox and dance floor, and only a few tables, which encouraged people to move around and meet others. Even so, groups of women tended to be segregated within the bar. The women whose behavior deliberately followed the butch and the more passive "femme" roles tended to separate themselves from those women who were not committed to playing these roles. Other divisions were based on the women's class, age, and ethnicity. In the 1970s, as the city's openly lesbian population increased, entrepreneurs opened new and more specialized establishments. The newer bars reflected a clear class hierarchy, from stylish private clubs with professional memberships to beer and pool halls with working-class patrons.[7]

Bars have been very significant in gay and lesbian life because they have provided the primary settings in which people could find companions and/or sex partners of the same sex. In workplaces or neighborhood stores, homosexuals had to work hard to hide this aspect of their lives, which made it very difficult (and risky) for them to find each other. If you were a lesbian and thought another woman was also, you would have to go through "lengthy verbal games, dropping subtle hints . . . waiting for her to pick up your clues before you dared to reveal yourself."[8] None of this was necessary in a lesbian or gay bar, and prior to the development of homosexual enclaves, such bars were the only places where people of the same sex could talk, touch, and dance; "cruise" in search of sexual partners; and openly interact as homosexuals. Thus, these bars were the one kind of environment that could provide homosexuals with a territorial referent, or sense of place.

Given the centrality of gay and lesbian bars to homosexual life, visiting these bars has often been an important "coming out" experience. Going to such a bar meant crossing a symbolic line, translating a private identity into public interaction. One man was 32 years old before he took this step, but he remembered it vividly five years later. His first terror, which struck him as he drove to the bar, involved his car. "Oh, my God," he thought, "I hope nobody sees my car because they'll know right where I'm going." He found a place to park across the street from the bar but then just sat there with the car doors locked. To go in, or not to go in, he deliberated. "I just knew there would be somebody in the bar I knew." Finally, after about thirty minutes he ran across the street, but glancing back, he noticed that he had left his car lights on and returned to the car. The anxiety came back and he sat inside the car again for a while. Eventually, he once again gathered his nerve, walked across the street, and went into the bar.[9]

Homosexuals' fear of coming out, especially during the decades right after World War II, resulted from their knowledge of the sanctions they could typically expect, which could include rejection by friends and family, eviction from housing, and termination of employment. There were also the "gay-bashing" forays organized by heterosexual gangs and the routine harassment by police, who periodically raided their bars and arrested patrons. Although homosexuals were tormented in San Francisco during this period, it was probably less severely than in most places. For example, California was one of few states not to prohibit congregations of homosexuals in public places. In New York State, by contrast, same-sex touching, dancing, or the like was classified as "degenerate" and punishable by fines or arrest.[10]

THE STONEWALL RIOTS

Because of the importance of gay bars in homosexuals' lives, police intrusion into these bars cut to the heart of gays' shared social life. However, police raids and bar closings, often based on frivolous grounds, were common. In almost every instance, patrons suffered their indignities quietly. Then came the Stonewall Inn riots, which turned out to be of national symbolic significance to the gay and lesbian movement. The Stonewall Inn was a small bar on Christopher Street in Greenwich Village, New York's closest approximation of Castro Street and the Castro district. The bar served a predominantly male, homosexual clientele, many of whom were described as "blatant queens in full drag."[11] These men wore shoes with four-inch heels, gowns, strings of pearls, wigs, and long painted fingernails.

On June 27, 1969, a small group of police tried to close the Inn. Forced closings were not an unusual occurrence, and patrons had not objected too strongly in the past. The police knew, as one drag queen later put it, that "little fairies never fight back."[12] This time, however, when the police threw the bartender and several "queens" into a paddy wagon, the mood of the crowd suddenly changed. People began to yell and boo. When the police next dragged out a struggling lesbian, bystanders began to throw bottles at the police. Facing the police, the gay men formed a chorus line, kicking and singing "We are the Stonewall girls." They then threatened to rape the policemen, who barricaded themselves inside the Inn. Several demonstrators uprooted a parking meter and used it as a battering ram on the door. The police turned a firehose on the crowd, which then temporarily dispersed. While the demonstrators were regrouping, several carloads of police reinforcements arrived, and the demonstrators disappeared. However, the next night, when a large police contingent returned to the area around Stonewall they confronted an "army" of middle-aged homosexuals, transvestites, teenage male prostitutes, a few lesbians, and some passersby. There was more bottle throwing, more marching and singing, and more arrests.

The resolve and defiance of the demonstrators at the Stonewall Inn became a rallying point for gay and lesbian organizations in many U.S. cities. In New York, an umbrella organization declared the anniversary of the street demonstrations "Christopher Street Liberation Day," which is celebrated by a week of art shows, dances, and a parade with gay and lesbian banners. In San Francisco, the anniversary is marked by the annual Gay Freedom Day Parade, which attracts hundreds of thousands of people.

The years following the Stonewall riots were characterized by an increase in the number of homosexuals who came out, seeking openly gay and lesbian lives, and by an increase in the size and strength of organizations pursuing gay interests in politics, religion, and other institutions.

With growing numbers of openly homosexual people interacting with each other, gay and lesbian cultures emerged, and it became possible to differentiate among homosexuals by their varying life-styles.

SEXUALITY AND LIFE-STYLE

The term *homosexual* is usually applied to people who engage in sexual acts with persons of the same sex. Such persons' intimate relations vary along a number of dimensions: They may or may not be exclusively homosexual, and the homosexual liaisons may be secret or known, frequent or sporadic, central to a person's identity or peripheral. To apply the same label (that is, *homosexual*) across this entire range of people and relations captures one quality they share, but it does not address the place of homosexuality in their lives. Put in other terms, *homosexual* can be viewed as an adjective because it describes some of the (sexual) things a person does; the terms *gay* and *lesbian* are often used as nouns because they describe who a person is.[13] Some writers also believe that the emphasis on sexual conduct is misplaced. In the view of some lesbians, it is the way they think, feel, and relate to each other that differentiates them from straights; they consider themselves most like straights in terms of their sexual behavior.[14]

Homosexuals have for many years lived under an oppressive fear of disclosure, which ensured that their social circles remained small, barely visible, and confined largely to furtive sexual contacts. If one goes back to the 1920s, at least in sections of New York City, some gay social circles were only half hidden. Homosexual men had codes for identifying each other (such as red ties), used certain parks and cafeterias as meeting places, and held large "drag balls" that attracted thousands of tourists and participants. It was not until the 1930s, historian George Chauncey argues, that sexual choices and identities came to be viewed in society as rigidly fixed, with little tolerance shown to those who deviated.[15]

In recent years many states and cities have passed laws extending civil rights protections so that homosexuality, per se, cannot be the basis for firing someone from a job, evicting a person from an apartment, or the like. These safeguards seem to be the result of organized political efforts by gays and lesbians rather than increasing acceptance of homosexuals by the general public.[16] However, the minimal safeguards extended to homosexuals, along with post-Stonewall feelings of assertiveness, have led to larger and more visible associations. Being a part of one of these groups is frequently very important to people, who pay the price for coming out—often, rejection by family and former friends. These new relationships replace those that are lost and afford an opportunity for homosexuals to play more inclusive gay and lesbian roles.[17]

Not all homosexuals make this transition, of course. Some continue to hide their sexual orientations and behavior, projecting an exclusively heterosexual social identity. Others do not deny their homosexuality but regard it as being confined to the sexual dimension of their lives, and they are attracted neither to local gay communities nor to gay culture. For example, one man's description of himself as a homosexual stressed his erotic fascination with masculinity. He has thought at length about the kinds of clothing and style that attract him to another man, and he has not tried to hide his many and diverse homosexual experiences. However, he does not identify with gay culture and does not feel his attitudes are like those of other men he thinks of as gay. Unlike himself, his description of them is that they are "men who live in a gay neighborhood, have gay friends, go to gay bars, and have a kind of specialized ghetto mentality."[18]

In a book about enclaves, we will of course be primarily focusing on people with gay or lesbian identities, because they are the core of gay and lesbian enclaves. It must also be recognized that even people with highly salient gay or lesbian identities differ from each other in such aspects as race, social class, and religion. They are not of a single social type, but space will not permit us to fully describe the variations.

GAYS IN THE CASTRO

The Castro district today is a middle-class residential neighborhood of apartments in renovated Victorian houses, many of which are pastel colored. It contains a typical commercial center with a full complement of clothing stores, banks, restaurants, and laundromats; and it houses the religious and political institutions that can be found in any community. The only thing out of the ordinary about the area is the fact that many of the residents and store owners are gay—and they are not trying to disguise it.

Until the late 1960s, the Castro was a somewhat run-down, Irish working-class neighborhood. An anomaly was the presence of two gay bars that had opened in the Castro to serve hippies from the nearby Haight–Ashbury district. Many in the traditional working-class Castro community were leaving during the 1960s because the factories in which they had been working had left the area; most of the local manufacturing jobs moved across the bay to Oakland or left the country entirely. Housing prices fell, attracting young homosexuals who "spilled over" from the Haight. During the 1960s Haight–Ashbury was a center of antiwar counterculture—"hippies." The heterosexual hippies were relatively tolerant of the homosexuals among them, and the homosexuals were relatively comfortable with the hippies' advocacy of peace, love, and nonconformity. Young, gay hippies were initially attracted to the Castro by cheap rents, but as the district's reputation as "a liberated zone" increased, they and nonhippie homosexuals were attracted by its social climate. During the mid-1970s, Castro property values began to rise, as an estimated 30,000 homosexuals from elsewhere in San Francisco and from around the country moved into the district.[19]

The resurgence of a declining neighborhood that results from an infusion of gays and lesbians has in more recent years become a familiar pattern across the country. It has been repeated in a number of other cities, as in Seattle's Capital Hill, Houston's Montrose section, Cincinnati's Liberty Hill, and Washington's Dupont Circle, to name just a few. In each case, a community in transition became the destination for gay and lesbian migrants, whose influx increased property values and who became increasingly open in their life-styles as their numbers increased. One gay rights advocate summed it up by saying, "We're here. We need a realtor."[20]

It was a diverse group of men who moved to the Castro during the 1970s. Included in it were gay physicians and psychologists, with specialties in treating gay patients; gay lawyers specializing in the types of discrimination and child custody cases experienced by gay men; a gay-owned savings and loan association that did not discriminate against gay applicants; and travel agencies and insurance brokers catering to the distinctive needs of a gay clientele. What they all had in common was a belief that the Castro was their refuge; a place to start life over without having to hide or deny their sexual preference. They also established religious congregations suited to their way of life. For example, the pastors of the Metropolitan Community Church performed gay marriages. In short, they built a self-contained gay community.

As the enclave grew during the 1970s, it offered men the sexual freedom to explore new kinds of homosexual relationships: some open and communal, some exclusive; some patterned after heterosexual relations and some not. "In the Castro," one resident said, "How you live together is a matter of negotiation."[21] For men who simply wanted as much homosexual sex without commitment as they could find, the Castro offered bathhouses, where any evening a man could anonymously pair off with as many other men as his stamina would allow. There were also numerous bars and even busy streets that were perfect for cruising. To grab another man's body was about as easy as getting a hamburger, which was why Castro residents called it "fast-food sex."[22]

"MAYOR" HARVEY MILK

One of the men who moved to the Castro to find himself in the early 1970s was Harvey Milk. An ex–New Yorker, at 42 years of age he opened a small camera store on Castro Street in 1973 and moved into an apartment above it.[23] His store was one of the first of the wave of gay-operated stores to move into the then-deteriorated working-class area. He thought the

Castro promised an interesting future because of its central location in the city, its charming nineteenth-century Victorians, and its cheap rents.

Over time, Milk's store devoted less space to camera supplies and more to notices, petitions, and brochures. Many of the issues were gay-related and arose as the gay newcomers clashed with the working-class holdovers. For example, the old-line store owners excluded the new gay businessmen from their meetings. In response, Milk helped to organize a new group, the Castro Village Merchants Association. He was openly gay, and advocated gay interests, but his concerns were not limited. He aggressively advocated more funding for public schools, libraries, and public transportation, among other things.

Milk, in sneakers and Levi's, with a thick black mustache and long hair in a ponytail, saw himself both as a street person and as the unofficial mayor of Castro Street. At age 43, for the first time in his life, Milk ran for public office. He lost the race for city council because voting was citywide, but he was the top vote getter in gay areas such as the Castro. He lost several more times before finally being elected as the Castro's city supervisor in 1977. In the course of his campaigns, Milk became a central figure in the neighborhood. He organized business associations and the annual Castro Street Fair; he rallied gay groups to economic and political issues with slogans such as "Gay Buy Gay" and "Gay Vote Gay;" and he forged alliances between the young gays, who were his core constituents, and a variety of other business, civic, and union organizations. As a result of his organizing ability he became an effective legislator, seeing through to passage a bill (which he introduced) that forbids discrimination against gays in housing and employment in San Francisco.

In 1978, Harvey Milk was one of two city supervisors who were shot and killed by a former supervisor. That night an estimated 40,000 people carrying candles, crying, and singing marched from the Castro to City Hall.[24] It was the end of Harvey Milk, the man—and also of his politics, because the Castro had dramatically changed during the 1970s. By 1978 the transition was largely complete. The Irish working-class families were virtually all gone; so too were the hippies. The interior and exterior of most of the housing had been renovated. Real estate values were doubling every six months, as gay tourists were coming from everywhere in the world to eat in Castro's gay restaurants and shop at its upscale gay men's clothing stores.

AIDS

It was shortly after Milk's death that AIDS became a focal issue in the gay community. As late as 1982, fewer than 100 cases per year of AIDS were diagnosed in San Francisco. But the numbers increased rapidly: to over 1,000 new cases diagnosed in 1985, over 3,000 in 1990, and a peak of over 3,300 cases in

1992. The Castro district has the highest AIDS rate in San Francisco, which, in turn, has the highest rate of any American city; and almost all of those infected in San Francisco are homosexual or bisexual men.[25]

As the epidemic spread, leaders of gay organizations looked inside and outside of the community for help. The U.S. government was urged to increase funding for HIV research and to speed the process by which new drugs for treating AIDS could be approved, but Castro residents generally perceived the government's response to be deficient. Looking to change behavior inside the community, several gay organizations, along with San Francisco public health officials, tried to convince gays to discontinue high-risk sexual practices. The bathhouses of the Castro were an obvious target, but one that divided the community. Engaging in anal intercourse with multiple partners and no condom—typical conduct in the bath-houses—seemed to many public health officials the single best way to spread AIDS, and they wanted the baths closed. Some local organizations such as the Harvey Milk Club agreed, and put out pamphlets warning men about high-risk practices. Other organizations, however, such as the Stonewall Gay Democratic Club, were suspicious of outsiders and were not prepared to give up any of their freedoms. The bath owners fought to remain open, and they were prepared to invest a lot in the battle because the bathhouses in the Castro were a big business, attracting both local gays and tourists.[26]

An important person in the conflict over the baths was Randy Shilts, previously cited as Harvey Milk's biographer. Shilts, who spent the last dozen years of his life as a reporter for the *San Francisco Chronicle,* was an openly gay activist, who in the early 1980s began writing about the AIDS peril. In his stories he was critical of the government, the medical establishment, and some gay organizations for their seeming indifference to the epidemic; and he urged that the baths be closed.[27] As the issue went through the courts in the mid-1980s, the baths were periodically closed and reopened, but the most significant by-product of the struggle was the educational campaign that began. Local organizations developed a number of model prevention programs that eventually proved highly effective. In 1993, the number of new AIDS cases in San Francisco dropped by 50 percent, even though the epidemic had not yet peaked in the rest of the nation; and the San Francisco Department of Public Health forecasted a continuing decline in the number of new cases every year until at least 1997.

Despite the recent decline in new cases, surveys suggest that high-risk sexual behavior may again be increasing, portending future increases in AIDS rates. Therapists in the Castro district offer a number of possible explanations. Some attribute men's disregard of the risks to depression brought on by so much death and suffering. "Depression is now a community norm," one said.[28] Another therapist reported that his Castro clients have lost so many loved ones that they fantasize about dying themselves in order to be reunited with them. For some men, AIDS has become so interwoven with life in the Castro that they regard getting the disease as a sign that they belong.

LESBIANS IN THE MISSION DISTRICT

About one mile to the east of Castro Street is the Mission district, which is one of several adjoining neighborhoods that are home to large numbers of lesbians living alone, in pairs, or in groups. These areas are also home to Hispanic, African American, and white ethnic families and to persons of varying wealth. In these racially and economically diverse areas, no single life-style or social type predominates. Housing is also mixed. There are a large number of older Victorian two- and three-story houses, in varying condition, modified to comprise two, three, four, and sometimes six flats. Intermixed with these are a few newer condominiums and apartment buildings.

Valencia Street in the Mission district is the retail and organizational center for the larger lesbian community. It contains a number of establishments that cater primarily to a lesbian clientele. For example, The Old Wive's Tales Bookstore stocks a wide range of specialty books by and about lesbians, and greeting cards written in a way that assumes both sender and recipient are women. The bulletin board in the bookstore functions as a kind of "town crier."[29] Posted on it are notices of apartments to rent, services being offered, and organizational meetings—all of which are intended for a lesbian audience. On the same block is a café whose former owners refused to admit men, and a shop that sells various artifacts made by women crafters. Valencia Street also contains a number of sexually oriented establishments, serving both local residents and tourists. The Good Vibrations store, for example, sells adult toys, books, videos, and so on, as their sign says, "especially for women." In addition, there are a number of lesbian bars in the neighborhood that offer adult entertainment such as lesbian burlesque shows, and there is Osento, the women's bathhouse.

Several women's services organizations are also housed on Valencia. Examples include The Lesbian Recovery Services Program and Women's Counseling Services. It should be noted, however, that most of these organizations serve a larger geographical area, and that other organizations for whom lesbians are the primary target group are also located in the Castro district and in other parts of San Francisco. Bay Area Career Women, for example, is a lesbian organization with an estimated 1,500 members from all parts of the city. The Lesbian Rights Task Force's recent directory of organizations serving lesbians in the San Francisco area was eight pages long.[30]

The Mission district and the neighborhoods adjoining it offer openly lesbian women the opportunity to associate primarily with others who are openly homosexual, or who are at least tolerant of lesbians. As one young woman explained, "My landlord is gay, my boss is gay, everyone I associate with is either gay or is used to dealing with gay people. . . . Nobody would say 'dyke' who wasn't one around here."[31] Within the Mission, violence is sometimes directed at lesbians, but women are generally able to express affection to each other in public without antagonizing observers. This aspect of the district was captured by a visitor who accompanied two residents of the Mission (Sandy and Jean) on a Saturday night outing. These two women lived together in a condominium just off Valencia Street, and one evening they took their guest to a neighborhood lesbian bar. She saw that downstairs was a narrow bar packed with hundreds of women, mostly single and looking, a few couples out to celebrate. Upstairs was a dance floor where women, mostly wearing sneakers and jeans and with extremely short blond hair, were dancing with each other. The three of them watched for a time, then left. Walking back down Valencia Street, Sandy grabbed Jean's hand, and held it aloft. "This is what it's all about!" Sandy cried. "We can walk . . . like this."[32]

To some degree the lesbian concentration in the Mission fits the definitional requirement of an enclave. There is a concentrated number of people in a residential area who share a distinctive quality. They feel attached to this area, and it houses specialized stores and institutions that serve the group. However, in other important respects, it is not a lesbian enclave. One ordinarily assumes that people who share a distinctive quality will predominate in any area that is considered their enclave, but only a small minority of the residents in the Mission and the adjoining areas (Noe Valley and Bernal Heights) are lesbians. Their identification with their particular area is also blunted by the whole city's openness to alternative life-styles. Thus, to some degree they (and some gays) identify more with the city of San Francisco than with their specific place of residence. Furthermore, the lesbian residential areas, including the commercial and institutional concentrations on Valencia Street, are lacking both the institutional and commercial self-sufficiency associated with enclaves.

Many of the "missing ingredients" are shared with the gay community and located in the Castro district. For example, Congregation Sha'ar Zahav is a small synagogue with an almost exclusively gay and lesbian membership. When writer Neil Miller visited it on a Friday night, it was filled, mostly with men wearing traditional skull caps, or *yarmulkes*. Shortly after the service began, the rabbi asked two women to come to the pulpit. He removed his prayer shawl and, with the help of a few others, held it over them. He was going to marry the two women the following week, and this was the traditional prenuptial blessing. The congregants chanted a traditional good luck phrase and threw candy at the couple, who kissed and then returned to their seats, and the service continued. Other shared institutions and activities located in the Castro are AIDS foundations and clinics, supported by both gay and lesbian groups; political action groups promoting gay and lesbian issues; and public rituals such as Halloween celebrations on Castro Street.

In sum, while the Mission district (with or without adjoining neighborhoods) does not qualify as a lesbian enclave, its residential concentration is too large and its commercial and institutional development too advanced to simply be dismissed. All things considered, the best conclusion is to regard the lesbian concentration in Mission as a subenclave of the Castro and to view the lesbian residential convergence in neighborhoods adjoining Mission as satellites of this subenclave, because of their dependence on Valencia Street commercial and institutional activities. The above distinctions between the Mission and Castro districts may also be temporary. When the Castro became an enclave during the 1970s there were very few women with experience in major institutional roles; few women religious leaders, political organizers, doctors and dentists, and so on. It would have been more difficult for any group of women at that time to establish a reasonably self-contained community. However, these gender differences are now disappearing, which may result in the Mission's ability to fulfill all the requirements for definition as an enclave.[33]

COALITIONS AND CONFLICTS

Facing similar hostility from the dominant "straight" society, gay and lesbian communities would seem likely coalition partners. In many instances they have been. There are organizations in place, such as the San Francisco Gay and Lesbian Bar Association, that promote both groups' common interest in political and legislative arenas. Each has also supported the other's candidates for elective office. For example, Harvey Milk received active backing from lesbian organizations, and Mary Morgan, a San Francisco Municipal Court Justice and the first openly lesbian judge in the United States, received strong support from the Castro.

There have also been some powerful gay–lesbian alliances in response to AIDS. Although lesbians have been relatively unaffected by the epidemic, they have been actively involved both to show solidarity with gays and to oppose right-wing claims that AIDS is God's way of eliminating homosexuals. Gay and lesbian groups worked together on such projects as safe-sex educational campaigns and fund-raising for AIDS treatment centers. To dramatize the need for government help and to symbolize the magnitude of the suffering, the Names Project of San Francisco, a gay and lesbian alliance, created a huge "AIDS quilt." Each square in the giant quilt, which was publicly displayed in many cities, represented a person who had died of AIDS.[34]

In San Francisco and several other cities, gays and lesbians also formed chapters of ACT-UP: AIDS Coalition To Unleash Power. In 1990, members of an ACT-UP group in New York who were looking for a broader basis for joint gay and lesbian action formed Queer Nation. Local chapters quickly followed in San Francisco and other cities. The term *queer*—most often used derisively by straights—was intentionally selected because it was confrontational, and an "in-your-face" organization was what the founders had in mind. They were also specifically looking for an umbrella term to cover both gays and lesbians. The initial membership consisted of people who were sick of justifying their existence to straight society and were not prepared to accept discrimination in any form. Their slogan is "Queers Bash Back," and one way they have tried to express this is by economically punishing businesses that discriminate against gays or lesbians.[35]

Queer Nation appeals to strong feelings in gay and lesbian communities, and its eventual success would further strengthen the tie between the two. However, fault lines appeared in this organization almost immediately, and they were the same kinds of rifts that have continuously inhibited coalitions between gays and lesbians in the past. Recurrent problems arise because people who are gay or lesbian can also be either young or old, black or white, rich or poor; these differences invariably lead some segment of the community to feel that its primary interests have been ignored by any organization. Queer Nation quickly came to be regarded by many lesbians and ethnic gays as especially suited to the needs of middle-class, white gays (the group that predominated in its founding). Groups feeling that they do not fit under any umbrella are a familiar problem in the Castro and the Mission.[36]

Along with the differentiation within each community, alliances have been hampered by attitudinal disagreements between gays and lesbians. Pornography has provided a particularly contentious issue, relating to fundamental value differences within and between the two groups. Some lesbian organizations have taken clear feminist positions that favor banning pornography, arguing that it is demeaning to women, promotes views of women as sexual objects, and encourages rape. Other lesbian groups hesitate to limit first amendment rights, and still others want to differentiate between the erotic (which they think is okay) and the violent (of which they disapprove). To most gay men, in contrast, pornography is valued for its potential to stimulate sexual activity, with such activity viewed as "play." They also regard pornography as useful in helping gays to liberate themselves from conventional socialization, which led them to view their "private parts" as dirty.[37]

Pornography has probably been a lightning rod because it touches on several underlying philosophical differences in gay and lesbian communities. Specifically, gays have often regarded lesbians as being too conservative sexually and having an exaggerated sense of political correctness. Correspondingly, lesbians have tended to view gays as being too preoccupied with sex and lacking social commitment. Neither argument is easy to prove, because of the previously noted differences in characteristics within each group. For instance, the concern with political correctness is probably stronger among middle-class, feminist lesbians than among working-class, nonfeminist lesbians. The belief that the cited differences between gays and lesbians exist is also based on events and experiences open to different interpretations. For example, one fund-raiser at the Castro Theater featured two acts: the Lesbian Chorus and Charles Pierce, a female impersonator. When Pierce began his routine, most of the women in the audience were offended and walked out, concluding that the gay men in the audience were insensitive.[38]

The notion that sexual aspects of homosexuality are more salient to gays than lesbians is also frequently contended, but again, difficult to prove. The assertion is consistent with the fact that lesbian bathhouses, which offer casual sex among numerous partners, have not flourished to the same extent as gay baths. On the other hand, it must be remembered that baths offer only one type of sexual contact. There are also congruent data that indicate that rates of sexual contact are substantially higher among gay than lesbian couples,[39] but survey data on this topic must be suspect because of the virtual impossibility of selecting samples that accurately represent the full array of gays and lesbians. Furthermore, there is some question as to whether gays and lesbians even mean the same thing when they report on how often they "have sex." Perhaps it is the number of male orgasms that is counted by gay and heterosexual couples; if so, lesbian couples would obviously have to use some other criterion.[40]

It is very difficult, of course, to predict what relations within and between gay and lesbian groups might be like in the future. What seems the most likely alternative is for splintering to continue along racial, ethnic, and life-style dimensions. Paradoxically, the very openness of the social climate in San Francisco (and other coastal cities), which facilitates the emergence of distinctive life-style groups, may simultaneously make it difficult for them to unite. New groups keep arising and differentiating themselves, feeling they do not fit under any established umbrella. To illustrate, one of the newest groups to emerge is that of bisexual women. Feeling estranged from heterosexuals but believing that lesbians "trivialized" their distinctiveness, they established a national bisexual network at a 1990 conference in San Francisco. By the end of 1992 they had established no fewer than thirty-one bisexual social and political organizations in the San Francisco area.[41]

NOTES

1. Frances FitzGerald, *Cities on a Hill,* New York: Simon & Schuster, 1986, p. 32.
2. Ibid., p. 33.
3. The proprietor of Maude's, Rikki Streicher, was also the creator of the Federation of Gay Games. See her obituary in *The New York Times,* August 24, 1994.

4. John D'Emilio, *Sexual Politics, Sexual Communities*, Chicago: University of Chicago Press, 1983.
5. Allan Berube, "Marching to a Different Drummer," in Martin Duberman et al. (Eds.), *Hidden from History*, New York: Meridian, 1989.
6. Lillian Faderman, *Odd Girls and Twilight Lovers*, New York: Columbia University Press, 1991.
7. Line Chamberland, "Remembering Lesbian Bars: Montreal, 1955–1975," *Journal of Homosexuality* 25, 1993. For a discussion of similar types of specialization in lesbian bars during this period, see Elizabeth L. Kennedy and Madeline D. Davis, *Boots of Leather, Slippers of Gold*, New York: Routledge, Chapman and Hall, 1993.
8. Faderman, op. cit., p. 163.
9. Frederick R. Lynch, "Nonghetto Gays," in Gilbert Herdt (Ed.), *Gay Culture in America*, Boston: Beacon Press, 1992, p. 174.
10. Warren J. Blumenfeld and Diane Raymond, *Looking at Gay and Lesbian Life*, Boston: Beacon Press, 1988.
11. Ibid., pp. 275–76.
12. Quoted in *The New York Times*, June 23, 1994, p. 1.
13. Michael Denneny, "Gay Politics," in Denneny et al. (Eds.), *The Christopher Street ReadeR*, New York: Coward-McCann, 1983. See also Stephen O. Murray, "Components of Gay Community in San Francisco," in Herdt (Ed.), op. cit.
14. This argument is explored in several interviews and personal essays included in Lily Burana et al. (Eds.), *Dagger: On Butch Women*, Pittsburgh: Cleis Press, 1994.
15. George Chauncey, *Gay New York*, New York: Basic Books, 1994.
16. With respect to males, for example, a national sample of 15- to 19-year-olds in 1988 reported that 89 percent strongly agreed that "men having sex with each other is disgusting." Furthermore, a large majority said they could not be friends with a gay person. William Marsiglio, "Attitudes Toward Homosexual Activity and Gays as Friends," *Journal of Sex Research* 30, 1993.
17. Margaret Cruikshank, *The Gay and Lesbian Liberation Movement*, London: Routledge, 1992. Cruikshank also argues that gay culture depends on reduced but continuing opposition to homosexuality, because it sharpens the sense of difference and the need of gays and lesbians to band together.
18. George Stambolian, "Interview with a Fetishist," in Denneny et al., op. cit., p. 160.
19. FitzGerald, op. cit.
20. Quoted in *The New York Times*, September 6, 1994, p. A14.
21. FitzGerald, op. cit., p. 55.
22. Andrew Holleran, "Fast-Food Sex," in Denneny et al., op. cit., p. 71.

23. The description of Milk that follows is based on Randy Shilts, *The Mayor of Castro Street*, New York: St. Martin's, 1982.

24. When Milk's assassin was convicted only of manslaughter, there was serious rioting in the Castro and open fighting between gays and police. One consequence was the San Francisco Police Department's recruitment of gay officers, most of whom were assigned to the Castro. See Neil Miller, *In Search of Gay America*, New York: Atlantic Monthly Press, 1989.

25. Consider the following 1993 comparisons: In San Francisco there were 280 cases of AIDS per 100,000 people; in New York City there were 155; in Youngstown, Ohio, 5. All of the preceding figures are from *The New York Times*, February 16, 1994, p. A10.

26. FitzGerald, op. cit.

27. His best-selling book on the slow response to AIDS, *And the Band Played On* (New York: St. Martin's Press, 1987), was nominated for a National Book Award and made into a 1993 movie. Ironically, Shilts tested positive for the HIV virus on the day he completed this book, and he died in 1994. See his obituary in *The New York Times*, February 18, 1994.

28. Quoted in *The New York Times*, December 11, 1993, p. 10.

29. Martha B. Barrett, *Invisible Lives*, New York: Harper & Row, 1990, Chapter Eight.

30. Cruikshank, op. cit.

31. Faderman, op. cit., p. 298.

32. Barrett, op. cit., p. 82.

33. The strongest argument for the existence of a more or less self-contained lesbian enclave with recognizable boundaries in San Francisco was presented by Deborah G. Wolf, *The Lesbian Community*, Berkeley: University of California Press, 1979. However, she focused primarily on one group of feminist lesbians, who would not constitute an enclave by our definition. Most authors conclude that a true lesbian enclave/community does not exist in San Francisco. See, for example, Ellen Lewin, *Lesbian Mothers*, Ithaca, NY: Cornell University Press, 1993.

34. Cruikshank, op. cit.

35. Faderman, op. cit., p. 301.

36. Kath Weston, *Families We Choose*, New York: Columbia University Press, 1991.

37. John Preston, "Goodby to Sally Gerhart," in Denneny et al., op. cit.

38. Miller, op. cit.

39. These findings were reported by Philip Blumstein and Pepper Schwartz, *American Couples*, New York: William Morrow, 1983.

40. See Marilyn Frye, "Lesbian 'Sex,'" in Jeffner Allen (Ed.), *Lesbian Philosophies and Cultures*, Albany: State University of New York Press, 1990.

41. Paula C. Rust, "Neutralizing the Political Threat of the Marginal Woman," *Journal of Sex Research* 30, 1993.

8

Hasidic Jews in Brooklyn

To outsiders, what is initially the most conspicuous feature of the Hasidim ("the pious ones") is their appearance. There are some variations among sects, but all women must for modesty's sake cover their bodies, which means heavy stockings and dresses (typically dark in color) that have long sleeves and high collars. Their heads, with hair cut short after marriage, are covered with kerchiefs or wigs. The men have full beards and ear-ringlet locks of hair, and they usually wear long black coats and black hats with wide brims and high crowns. Their clothing clearly sets them apart, and it is intended to; the Hasidim are vehemently opposed to assimilation. Most do not own television sets, and, in fact, many do not even speak English.

The Hasidic movement began in the Ukraine in the middle of the eighteenth century and grew to comprise over 1 million followers in Russia, Poland, and Hungary. The growth in the number of adherents was reversed by the Holocaust, in which most of the Hasidim perished. Many of the survivors resettled in the borough of Brooklyn, New York, near the end of World War II.

THE BROOKLYN NEIGHBORHOODS

In Brooklyn today there are three distinct Hasidic enclaves. Each contains a different mix of Hasidic sects, but there are overriding similarities among all of them. This chapter will focus primarily on the Lubavitch in Crown Heights. (Their name comes from the Russian city Lubavitch, where they were first organized.) We begin, however, with a brief overview of the three Brooklyn neighborhoods with Hasidic concentrations: Williamsburg, Crown Heights, and Borough Park.

Williamsburg is located at the northern edge of Brooklyn, just across the Williamsburg Bridge from Manhattan's lower east side. It is a community crowded with old brownstones, apartment buildings converted from

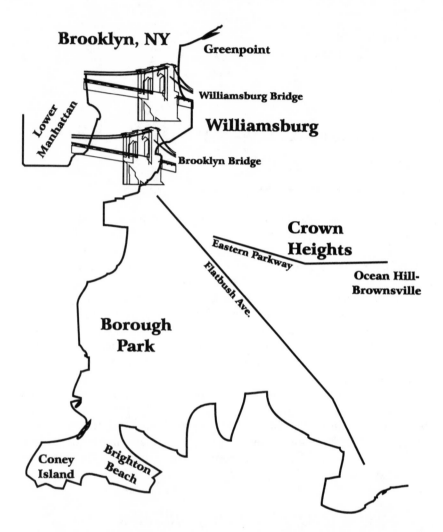

factories, and a few high-rise housing projects. Large numbers of Orthodox, but non-Hasidic, Jews lived in Williamsburg as early as the 1920s. Most left during the middle of the century as an estimated 65,000 Puerto Ricans and 35,000 Hasidic Jews moved in. Most of the latter were European immigrants who survived the Holocaust and resettled in New York near the end of World War II. The Hasidic community dominates the southwest section of Williamsburg, where it constitutes nearly three-quarters of the population. It is served by family-owned stores that sell food, clothing, and books, and holds the religious facilities of Satmar, the largest sect, and those of several smaller sects. There are also a variety of clinics, physicians, and psychiatrists that cater to the distinctive needs of the Hasidic population.

Crown Heights is located in the center of Brooklyn, about three miles south of Williamsburg. The Hasidic community in this neighborhood also originated from the relocation of Holocaust survivors at the end of World War II. Crown Heights is densely settled, with three-story brick buildings and two-story townhouses, a lot of which are in run-down condition. Of the approximately 15,000 Hasidim in Crown Heights, about 10,000 are Lubavitch. The center of their Brooklyn enclave, on Eastern Parkway, is their world headquarters: an imposing red brick building with bars over its windows for protection. In terms of population, the Hasidim are dwarfed by the estimated 160,000 black residents of Crown Heights, who are both African American and West Indian. Despite their vast differences in life-style, food, and dress, many live on the same streets in Crown Heights, sometimes in the same apartment buildings. However, the Hasidim maintain their distance, and relations between them and their neighbors are frequently strained.

Borough Park is the third enclave, located in the southwest corner of Brooklyn, about four miles from Crown Heights. It contains two-story apartment buildings, high-rise dwellings with terraces overlooking the Manhattan skyline, and some 100-year-old mansions that have been converted to apartments. The principal commercial street in Borough Park, 13th Avenue, houses a large assortment of relatively new restaurants, candy stores, and bookstores. Few Hasidic families lived in this neighborhood until the mid-1960s, when there were sizeable migrations from Williamsburg and, to a lesser extent, from Crown Heights. Some who moved there were attracted to Borough Park's better housing, others feared rising crime rates in their former neighborhoods, and still others merely wanted to remain close to family members who were moving. Ties between members of the same sects in different communities remained close; for example, the largest sect, Satmar, instituted private bus service for its members between Williamsburg and Borough Park. However, Borough Park is seen by many Hasidim as offering shopping and restaurants that are too upscale; it is sometimes criticized for providing too modern and too secular an environment. One Williamsburg resident said he would not want to live in Borough Park. "Over there . . . you have more women driving cars . . . ; over there you hear kids speaking English."[1]

HASIDIC RELIGIOUS VIEWS

The founders of the Hasidic movement attempted to reach out to the masses of Jews with a nonintellectual message that stressed the importance of simple devotion in leading to spiritual elevation. They were charismatic leaders, who extolled prayer, song, and comradeship. Each major Hasidic figure continues to be widely regarded by his followers as very special: a genius, a person capable of miracles and prophecies. His powers, most believe, might be able to hasten the coming of the long-awaited Messiah, who will be sent by God to provide righteousness and redemption. Perhaps their rebbe might even be ultimately revealed to be that Messiah. More conventional, mainstream rabbinical leaders tend to be highly critical of the strong mystical element in Hasidic beliefs, and opposed to what they consider to be Hasidic personality cults that offer false messianic visions.[2]

A majority of Jews (and gentiles) see the dress and customs of the Hasidim as strange anomalies in modern times. Some privately view the Hasidim as "ethnic embarrassments." However, giving public voice to these sentiments often inspires greater solidarity among Jews and provokes rebukes to the speaker. For example, the executive director of the American–Israel Public Affairs Committee, a non-Hasidic Jew, described the Hasidim as "smelly" and "low class" with a "poor immigrant image," and he said he was pleased never to have been to their Brooklyn enclaves.[3] When, in response, both secular and fundamentalist Jews besieged the board with complaints, he was forced to resign.

The Hasidim's lives are circumscribed by 613 *mitzvot*—commandments that they share with all Jews. Examples include observing the Sabbath, giving to charity, and eating only kosher food. Unlike other Jews, however, they believe that failure to observe the *mitzvot* can literally cause catastrophe for the negligent individual or the entire community. Furthermore, to be a Hasid entails zealously going beyond the letter of the law, as their observation of the Sabbath illustrates. The Hebrew Sabbath extends from just before sundown Friday to just after sundown Saturday. Observance requires ritual lighting of candles, special prayers, and prohibitions on activities such as working, traveling in vehicles, turning anything on or off, and carrying objects. Hasidic compliance is so literal and precise that they will not take jobs whose hours might ever conflict with observance of the Sabbath. They do not consider this much of a sacrifice; quality of life for Hasidim does not depend on material possessions.

By midafternoon Friday the streets of Crown Heights are filled with men in black suits and hats hurrying to prayer services at the Lubavitch synagogue. The places where they are employed in large numbers, such as the 47th Street diamond exchange in Manhattan, appear deserted. During other parts of the week, Hasidim can regularly be seen moving briskly between stores and offices in the diamond exchange carrying black sample cases. By three o'clock on Friday afternoons, however, the streets are nearly empty as the Hasidim make certain their travel is complete before sundown, when the Sabbath begins.[4] At the same time, women with baby carriages and arms full of grocery bags are hurrying home to prepare the Sabbath dinner. Young girls help their mothers in the kitchen, and young boys tape the light switches in the house to make sure none are accidently pushed on or off.[5]

In addition to differences in degrees of observance, Hasidim have also been separated from most American Jews by the formers' lack of support for Israel. The Hasidic emphasis on the coming of the Messiah has led many of them to take an antagonistic attitude toward the state of Israel, in marked contrast to non-Hasidic Jews, who tend to be extremely supportive of Israel as a Jewish, but secular, state. Some Hasidic groups believe that the Holy Land should be restored to Jews only by the Messiah. The Zionist movement, in their view, preempts God's role and, by violating the Messianic prophecy, may actually delay redemption. Other Hasidic groups might be prepared to accept the establishment of the State of Israel as signaling the beginning of redemption, were it not for the fact that it is a secular society that has sometimes permitted bus service on the Sabbath, archaeological digs in ancient grave sites, secular schools, and so on.[6]

In addition to the emphasis on the Messiah, a central Hasidic conception, according to philosopher Mordechai Rotenberg, entails the distinction between form and matter and a belief that they are integrally related. This dichotomy applies to several referents, one of which involves types of people. The "people of form" are the scholars, the moral leaders, who bestow spirituality upon the community. They require support from the "people of matter," who provide for the material needs of the collectivity. The survival and salvation of the entire community is believed to require the interconnectedness of its body (matter) and soul (form).

The distinction between form and matter and their necessary interconnectedness also pertains to psychological states within people, namely their spiritual and material selves. The individual seeks a state of redemption by combining community and material attachments with individual spiritual meditation. For example, to feel real spiritual joy, singing and dancing are considered helpful in "warming up" the material body and in spreading a feeling of elation among participants. Through the interconnectedness of form and matter, each individual hopes to spiritually ascend to a higher level of self-realization in which he may know God more fully. In this process the Hasid is admonished to "put himself as one who is not ... in this world."[7] The founder of the Hasidic movement is described as having trembled during prayers when he was inspired, his face burning like a torch, eyes bulging and fixed like a person in the throes of death.

THE REBBES

Each community of Hasidic Jews, from as few as 100 families to over 5,000 families, has historically been tied to a particular place in which their leader, a rebbe, establishes his "court." If the membership grows too large, new residential communities can form, but they remain tied to the same rebbe. The rebbe is the ultimate authority on both secular and religious matters. A Hasidic rabbi, by contrast, is an expert in ritual law who decides what behavior can be permitted under varying conditions. The rabbi also officiates at weddings and funerals and periodically addresses the congregation. He may be held in high regard, but a Hasidic rabbi is not presumed to possess the spiritual power or mystical insights of a rebbe.

At least once a year all the followers of a rebbe will come to seek his blessing. Those who live close by may see him regularly. For example, every Sunday morning at his Crown Heights residence, Rebbe Schneerson individually greeted thousands of his Lubavitch followers. They filed past him, and to each one he gave a crisp dollar bill and a blessing. The dollar was to encourage them to give to charity. Followers also seek the aid of their rebbe with "petitions" that present problems they are facing, such as a sick child or loss of a job. Most petitioners are men. Although a woman may speak to the rebbe, he will not shake her hand or look directly at her. She is expected to stand to the side of her husband, and he, as head of the family, faces the rebbe directly.

The rebbe may respond to a petitioner by simply giving some general assurance and offering a blessing. However, the petition asks the name of the follower's mother so that the rebbe can trace the lineage of the petitioner's soul and pray for resolution at the root of the problem. Because the prayers of rebbes are believed to fly upward unimpeded, they can intercede on behalf of their followers in Heavenly Court. Even when the assistance of a physician or other secular specialist is recommended by the rebbe for a specific problem, the prayers of the rebbe are still always considered to be necessary and of maximum importance.[8]

Allegiance to a particular rebbe is traditionally passed on within a family, but some especially charismatic rebbes attract new members. Many of the rebbes have international followings, with "branches" in a number of countries. In the outskirts of Tel Aviv, for example, a group of Israeli Lubavitch in 1990 built an exact replica of their world headquarters in Crown Heights. It even includes the Brooklyn address—770 Eastern Parkway—in large letters over the front door. A rebbe's court on any given day may have an international constituency, even though everyone looks the same, dressed in the garb of that particular sect. The rebbe is therefore in a position somewhat like the chief executive of a multinational corporation, having to make such global decisions as whether a new school should be built in Montreal or in Philadelphia. In addition, because most marriages occur within the sect, rebbes face additional questions not confronted by chief executives, such as, Should the newly married couple reside in the bride's or the groom's country? What would be best for the sect? What would be best for the families?[9]

The importance of a rebbe to his followers is indicated by the reactions of the Lubavitchers when Rebbe Schneerson became critically ill and died in the spring of 1994. He suffered a stroke and heart attack in March and was brought to a New York hospital. A dozen young men and their teachers convened daily in the hospital's chapel, splitting their days between a vigil for the rebbe's health and continuing their schoolwork. (Their studies were largely devoted to the rebbe's writings.) Thousands of his followers held rallies in a nearby park and Sabbath services in the hospital's auditorium. For weeks, the fragile, 92-year-old rebbe grew steadily weaker, but they continued to expect him to make a miraculous recovery.[10]

Despite their faith and prayers he died in May. Lubavitchers from Canada, Europe, and Israel immediately chartered planes and flew to New York for his funeral. His coffin was carried out of their Crown Heights headquarters by twenty men as an estimated 12,000 grief-stricken people watched. Women wailed and hugged each other. Men prayed and cried and pushed over police barricades in an effort to touch his coffin. Many regarded him as their personal spiritual mentor and felt "orphaned" by his death. Weeks after he was buried, thousands continued to leave notes for the rebbe on his grave. Some of the Lubavitch faithful had long been sure that Rebbe Schneerson was God's messenger, the Messiah, and he had only mildly discouraged this belief. "We are certain he will . . . be resurrected," claimed the rabbi who headed the Lubavitch Youth Organization. Now that he is "out of the body," claimed another Lubavitch rabbi, there are "no more limitations" on what he may accomplish.[11]

The fact that he did not recover and that he was not resurrected did not seem to disillusion his followers. Some believed that he was in another realm, still watching out for them. Others claimed that when the world was ready, he would return and prove to be the Messiah. The Hasidim reacted like other devout religious groups have customarily responded when their prophecies seem not to be confirmed. Adherents typically offer interpretations that rearrange events in a way that explains away any appearance of a contradiction. Their faith, as a result, is left intact or actually strengthened by the "failed" prophecy.[12]

One full year after his death, the Lubavitchers have still not replaced Rebbe Schneerson. Their spokesmen insist he will continue to be their rebbe until the Messiah comes, and they flock to his grave in Queens. Visitors from around the world, in buses and in cars, make pilgrimages to his graveside, where they claim they can still feel his presence hovering above his grave. The Queens cemetery in which Schneerson is buried is in a predominantly black, non-Jewish neighborhood, and the influx of Hasidic visitors has sometimes felt like an invasion to the residents. Some resented the intrusions of men in black fedoras and women in long dresses; but most of the people in the neighborhood were more perplexed than angry. One elderly resident said she did not understand what they were doing at the rebbe's grave. "Maybe they are waiting for him to rise," she guessed, then concluded, "I think they're going to have a long wait."[13]

A REBBE'S COURT

The principal structures of a rebbe's court consist of his home, where he accepts visitors; the synagogue and *yeshiva* (school); and the *mikvah* (ritual bath). There may also be other facilities, such as a library, summer camp, or neighborhood property; and any or all of these structures and facilities can be collectively owned by the community or held in the name of the rebbe. Schneerson, for example, owned everything and, when he died, left all to the Lubavitch council.

THE *YESHIVA*

A central part of every Hasidic community is one or more *yeshivas,* or schools. The Hasidim, who do not practice birth control, often have extremely large families, forcing communities to continuously add *yeshivas* unless some of the membership moves to another neighborhood. The study halls of large *yeshivas* are also used by members for services, thereby serving as synagogues.

Hasidic males and females are always kept separate, and school is no exception. Girls have traditionally received a limited religious and secular education in the community's girls' school, consistent with the domestic role that is expected to dominate their lives as adults. More recently, some sects have enlarged the educational opportunities they offer to women. Postsecondary training is now offered to young Bobover women in Borough Park, for example. Correspondingly, there has been some expansion in the kind of work considered appropriate for Bobover women, and within the community they have found work as teachers in the sect's nursery school and kindergarten.[14]

Larger *yeshivas* have long encompassed diverse educational levels for boys, and the most able young men continue their studies in a Talmudic college. From the high-school level on, boys begin fourteen-hour school days at 7:30 A.M., with breaks for meals and recreation. For part of a typical day, the boys attend lectures. However, most of their time is spent reading and discussing traditional religious laws and their interpretation, as well as Hasidic philosophy. Younger and older students study and discuss the material together and with the teachers and rabbis that work with them. Because the different groupings of students share close quarters, and their discussions tend to be animated, the *yeshiva* atmosphere is frequently tumultuous. Secular and religious study are combined, the mix of each varying by sect, but preparation for a religious life as a Hasidic Jew is always emphasized.

Prayers are recited three times daily—four times on Sabbath and festivals. During prayers, students concentrate and pray with reverence for themselves, their families, and the entire nation. Books in hands, they repeatedly bend over then straighten, their heads and bodies bobbing and swaying. These ritual movements have recently been associated with the extremely high incidence of myopia among advanced *yeshiva* students. The continual change of focus as their eyes move closer and farther from the books they hold while they bend and straighten during prayers is the apparent reason that most of them wind up wearing glasses.[15]

Learning is highly revered among the Hasidim. A boy's quality as a student is an important factor in determining his status in the community. If he is an accomplished student, that highly desirable quality will be emphasized, for example, by the matchmaker who seeks his future bride. In fact, many newly married Hasidic women who work outside the home do so primarily to permit their husbands to devote themselves full-time to continuing their (nonvocational) religious training.

A boy's education is almost always carried out within the *yeshiva* of his family's rebbe's court. This helps to maintain the closed boundaries of the community, and facilitates the boy's transition from school to community. Occasionally, however, an especially inspiring rabbi or rebbe may attract students from a different court. The problems created by such "conversions" are profound. Within what community will a marriage be arranged? And symbolically, sons are dramatically separated from their parents by not following the traditional allegiances of the family. In fact, to change *yeshivas* can be viewed as failing to honor one's father and mother, and some parents respond by holding funeral rites for their apostate sons, permanently ending all contact with them.[16]

THE *MIKVAH*

A *mikvah* is a ritual bath that resembles a very small indoor pool. It is usually located in a nondescript building that contains dressing rooms and the bath itself. Immersion in the lukewarm water is considered generally beneficial, uplifting one's spirits, relieving muscular pains, sometimes even enabling cripples to walk again. An immersion is highly recommended for men prior to certain holidays, and is one of a handful of rituals that is absolutely prescribed for women every month in conjunction with their menstrual cycles.

A woman is considered unclean for the length of her menstrual period and at least seven days thereafter. She remains in this state until she immerses herself in the *mikvah*. Every month, for this twelve-day (or longer) interval, any type of sexual relations between husband and wife are strictly prohibited. The ban even extends to actions that could arouse sexual desire; for example, sleeping in the same bed. (Sexual relations between unmarried persons are never permitted. An unrelated man and woman are not even allowed to be alone together in the same room.)[17]

After her period is over, a typical Hasidic woman walks to the *mikvah* and enters an outer room, in which she waits with other women. When it is her turn, she is taken by an attendant to a private room, where she very carefully and thoroughly bathes her entire body, even using cotton swabs for difficult-to-reach places. When she is done she puts on a white robe and presses a buzzer. An attendant comes to escort her to the bath. There she removes the robe and descends into the water. With feet apart and eyes open she slowly crouches until her body is completely immersed. Then, standing, she covers her head with a small white towel, recites a prayer in Hebrew, and immerses herself twice more. The attendant then helps her out of the bath and she returns to her dressing room.

Observing the extended menstrual ban and the ritual cleansing is viewed by the Hasidim as enabling a married couple to strengthen the non-sexual bonds that should tie them to each other along with sexual bonds. A balance between the two types of attachment is valued by the Hasidim, who believe that if the balance is upset, unborn children can be adversely affected. For example, one Hasidic woman mentioned the retarded child of a local couple and noted that his birth had "raised suspicions in the community."[18]

Although immersion is not rigidly prescribed for Hasidic men, many believe it fosters unity among them and elevates one's level of spirituality during prayer. The Hasidic movement's founding rebbe said that regular immersion may be even better for spirituality than a day of fasting. And one of his disciples said that a person who immerses in the morning will be seen by God as equivalent to a person who has fasted for the day.[19]

OUTREACH PROGRAMS

In most sects, the rebbe's courts are insular, almost exclusively oriented toward serving their own members. The Lubavitch, however, through the Chabad movement, have actively tried to promote religious orthodoxy among nonobservant Jews, and sometimes also tried to entice them to join Lubavitch communities. In the more than forty years he served as rebbe, Schneerson instructed his followers that they were charged with loving their fellow Jews, even the rebellious ones. Helping these nonreligious Jews adopt an observant life-style, he said, was their mission, and their success would hasten the coming of the Messiah. Groups of bearded young Lubavitch men, often wearing conventional business suits, spread out across New York from the Crown Heights headquarters. Many were college students at the Lubavitch *yeshiva* and Rebbe Schneerson viewed them also as soldiers in a military-type campaign. For example, they were driven to neighborhoods with large Jewish populations in order to proselytize in vans called "*mitzvah* tanks against assimilation."[20]

One Russian-Jewish immigrant, who had not practiced Judaism in Russia, returned to his New York home one evening and announced with a grin that he had a bar mitzvah that day. "Right on Fifth Avenue. Seriously! Really! Right in the middle of Manhattan on its most famous street!"[21] He had simply been walking down the street when he passed by a group of Lubavitchers standing in front of their van. They asked him if he was Jewish. When he said yes, they asked him if he would like to do a good deed. When he said yes again, they began his bar mitzvah service. Who ever heard of such a thing, he asked?

The Lubavitch outreach programs are run out of the sect's Crown Heights headquarters, a converted 1930s mansion. It and the adjacent building contain—in addition to the rebbe's offices, the *yeshiva,* and the synagogue—an educational center, a print shop, video equipment, and editorial and translation centers for disseminating the rebbe's messages around the world. Prospective new members are brought for visits to the headquarters and surrounding community. Around the time of major holidays, when sect members may come from anywhere in the world, the streets around the headquarters become so crowded that police are sent to direct traffic.

SOLIDARITY AND CONFLICT

Within the Hasidim's Brooklyn neighborhoods, the similarities in their appearance and way of life stand out, especially in contrast to their African American, West Indian, and Puerto Rican neighbors. Members of different sects have usually been willing to shop at each other's stores, exchange neighborly favors, and let their children play with each other. These informal contacts have promoted cohesion among different sect members living in the same neighborhoods. Members of all sects in every neighborhood have also been bound together by umbrella organizations established to promote their common interests in Brooklyn and New York City politics. Cohesion among the Hasidic sects has also been promoted by periodic conflicts between the individual sects and their non-Hasidic neighbors.

There have also, however, been periodic conflicts between sects, and the outreach programs of the Lubavitchers have frequently been the cause. The most serious long-term tensions have been between the Lubavitch and the Satmar sect in Williamsburg. During the Passover holiday, for example, the Lubavitchers used to visit other sects' synagogues to present their distinctive philosophy. To Satmar Hasidim, these visits were both unnecessary and provocative. In 1977, during Passover, hundreds of Lubavitch marched the three miles from Crown Heights to Williamsburg. When they arrived, Satmar members responded by shouting, spitting, and throwing garbage cans at the marchers. Fistfights broke out between the groups, who eventually had to be separated by the police. The Lubavitch then ended their Passover marches, and even rerouted their *mitzvah* tanks around Williamsburg.

Smaller confrontations have continued, however, with Lubavitch outreach activities usually providing the initial spark. For example, members of Satmar claimed that the Lubavitchers were intentionally using charismatic teachers to convert young Satmar males to Lubavitch views. During the mid-1980s, one such Lubavitch teacher was meeting with a Satmar teenager in the back of the youth's father's store. Five Satmar men were accused of running into the room as the lesson began, throwing the teacher (a rabbi) down on the floor, holding him there, and cutting off his beard. It was not only a physical assault but a spiritual blow, because of the Hasidic prohibition on shaving. In response, the Lubavitch banned consumption of all Satmar products, claiming they were no longer kosher.[22]

Relations between the Lubavitch and their non-Hasidic neighbors have usually been distant, and sometimes hostile. Like other sects, the Lubavitch typically avoid contact with outsiders, and even consider observant but non-Hasidic Jews to be outsiders. Their black Crown Heights neighbors, African American and West Indian, have sometimes felt that these "distant" Lubavitchers received preferential treatment in the community; for example, when major streets are closed off and police are assigned to traffic control around their Crown Heights headquarters during major holidays.

Resentment over local issues combined with growing black anti-Semitism to produce a violent riot following a tragic automobile accident on August 19, 1991. That evening, Rebbe Schneerson was returning home with a number of other Hasidim in a three-car procession with a police escort. One of the cars in the motorcade struck another car, then swerved onto the sidewalk, striking two (black) Guyanese children. One, a 7-year-old boy, died at the scene. As a crowd gathered, the driver of the errant car and his passengers, none of whom were seriously injured, were removed from the area by a private ambulance.

During the evening of the nineteenth, hostile suppositions spread through the West Indian and African American communities. (The two groups were unified by the racial polarization that resulted after the accident.) It was rumored, for example, that the black Guyanese youngster was callously left by the Hasidic ambulance to die. And because a police car had been leading the rebbe's motorcade, providing further evidence of the Hasidim's preferential treatment by the city, many black residents of Crown Heights doubted that those responsible for the boy's death would be punished. Over the next four days, there were confrontations between blacks and Jews in Crown Heights, and groups of angry young black men marched down Crown Heights streets chanting, "Kill the Jews!" One young

Hasidic man was stabbed to death the evening of the nineteenth, and other beatings of Jews by blacks occurred on the following days. Black groups also burned or looted a number of Hasidic-owned businesses.[23]

The adequacy of the police response to the Crown Heights disturbances was a matter of some contention. Eventually, over 1,000 police patrolled the streets, and hundreds of arrests were reported. However, the Hasidim and many other (especially white) New York residents were very critical of the police response, claiming it was too little too late. The city's first elected African American mayor, in the beginnings of a reelection campaign, was accused variously of favoritism, of timidity, or of being out of touch with what was happening. Criticism grew even stronger when the police investigation of the fatal stabbing was later shown to be sloppy, and the young African American man arrested for the murder was acquitted.

All the major Hasidic sects in New York lobbied elected representatives, urging that the U.S. Attorney General reopen the case. City officials, congressional representatives from Brooklyn, and New York State's two senators were all supportive. Eventually, the U.S. Senate passed a resolution urging further inquiry, and nearly three years later the man who had been acquitted on murder charges was rearrested on the federal charge of violating the victim's civil rights.[24]

After the rioting, a precinct council, a conflict resolution task force, a day-care program, and various other associations were proposed to bring the African American, West Indian, and Hasidic groups together. The three groups are alike in that they all have relatively large numbers of low-income families. Perhaps all could benefit from participating in a common program that would have a unifying effect. However, none of the umbrella associations have had more than limited and short-term success, and the different groups continue to be periodically driven apart by everyday conflicts. For example, in 1994, Labor Day fell on the eve of the Jewish New Year (Rosh Hashanah), when thousands of Hasidim travel to Lubavitch headquarters on Eastern Parkway. However, for over twenty-five years Labor Day has been the scheduled date for a Caribbean parade down Eastern Parkway; a parade that attracts over 1 million people. The Hasidim thought the Caribbean organizers should change the date of their event in 1994, and when those planning the parade refused, the Hasidim thought they were unreasonable. When Lubavitch representatives tried to get the police to change the date of the parade permit, the Caribbean organizers in Brooklyn were enraged.[25]

The animosities from the 1991 riot also remain, in part because the unsolved murder continues to be a divisive issue. As the federal investigation proceeded, thousands of black youths were questioned by police. This contributed to blacks' feelings that they are harassed by police in Crown Heights, and that the Hasidim receive preferential treatment. Many blacks also expect the 7-year-old boy who was killed by the Hasidic driver to be forgotten and some black man to be sacrificed in the name of justice. The older brother of the 7-year-old who was killed predicted, "If another trial happens and someone is found guilty, I think there will be riots again."[26]

The conflicts between the Lubavitch and their black neighbors have sometimes contributed to solidarity among the Hasidim, regardless of sect. At the same time, some members of other sects who have themselves had unpleasant encounters with Lubavitchers have quietly wondered how much the Lubavitch share the blame for provoking the 1991 riots. However, the shooting of four Lubavitch *yeshiva* students, in March 1994, immediately led to unambiguous sect solidarity. In that event, a Lebanese national named Rashid Baz was accused of firing into a van carrying *yeshiva* students from a hospital visit to Rebbe Schneerson. As they crossed the Brooklyn Bridge, the suspect apparently opened fire on the van, killing one teenager, gravely injuring another, and slightly wounding two others. Police interrogation produced no specific motive for the attack. It appeared an act of random violence. At a City Hall briefing for a diverse group of Jewish leaders the next day, Satmar and Lubavitch representatives sat side by side, and were joined by non-Hasidic Jewish leaders. All were united, at least for the time being, because the targets of the violence had apparently been selected solely because they were conspicuously Jewish.[27]

NOTES

1. Jerome R. Mintz, *Hasidic People*, Cambridge, MA: Harvard University Press, 1992, p. 111.
2. David Landau, *Piety and Power*, New York: Hill & Wang, 1993.
3. *The New York Times*, June 29, 1993, p. A10.
4. Robert M. Kamen, *Growing Up Hasidic*, New York: AMS Press, 1985.
5. Philip Baldinger, "Equality Does Not Mean Sameness," in Philip L. Kilbride et al. (Eds.), *Encounters with American Ethnic Cultures*, Tuscaloosa: University of Alabama Press, 1990.
6. Mintz, op. cit.
7. Mordechai Rotenberg, *Dialogue with Deviance*, Lanham, MD: University Press of America, 1993, p. 165.
8. Mintz, op. cit.
9. Landau, op. cit.
10. *The New York Times*, May 13, 1994, p. B3.
11. *The New York Times*, June 14, 1994, p. B1.
12. For a review of theories and studies, see Robert P. Althauser, "The Paradox in Popular Religion," *Social Forces* 69, 1990.

13. Quoted in *The New York Times,* March 11, 1995, p. 26.
14. Kamen, op. cit.
15. Landau, op. cit.
16. See Mintz, op. cit.
17. To avoid close contact with women during rush hours on New York subways, when Hasidic men work in concentrated numbers, such as at the diamond exchange, they use the sect's school buses. Some of the buses are even designed for morning and afternoon prayer services. See Kamen, op. cit.
18. Baldinger, op. cit., p. 168.
19. Aaron Werthheim, *Law and Custom in Hasidim,* Hoboken, NJ: Ktav Publishing House, 1992.
20. Mintz, op. cit., p. 45.
21. Fran Markowitz, *A Community in Spite of Itself,* Washington, DC: Smithsonian Institution Press, 1993, p. 163.
22. Mintz, op. cit.
23. For a chronology of the events leading to the Crown Heights rioting, see the preface to Anna D. Smith, *Fires in the Mirror,* New York: Anchor Books, 1993; and William M. Kephart and William W. Zellner, *Extraordinary Groups,* New York: St. Martin's, 1994.
24. For a summary of events following the initial acquittal, see *The New York Times,* August 12, 1994, p. B2.
25. *The New York Times,* January 27, 1994, p. B8.
26. Ibid.
27. *The New York Times,* March 4, 1994, p. B2.

9

Suburbanization, Multiculturalism, and Localization

In this chapter we will explore several issues that transcend any of the specific enclaves discussed in the rest of the book. We will begin by examining one of the major changes to have occurred in enclaves over the past 50 to 100 years, namely, their growth in suburban sites. In contemporary metropolitan areas, enclaves are located in both cities and suburban areas, whereas formerly they were almost exclusively located in inner cities. Simultaneous to the growth in suburban enclaves has been a growing emphasis within society on multiculturalism, which may affect the formation and permanence of enclaves and is our next topic. Finally, we will discuss how the commercial and institutional activities of enclaves—customized for local residents—run counter to a powerful societal movement towards uniformity and standardization, as exemplified by the growth of franchises.

SUBURBANIZATION AND MULTICULTURALISM

From roughly the 1870s to the 1970s, enclaves were typically located in or near the centers of cities. With increasing assimilation and economic attainments, residents left enclaves and moved farther out toward the periphery of cities. Less well-off newcomers took the others' former places and formed new enclaves in the center of the city. In the last twenty-five to thirty years, in contrast, many religious, racial, and life-style groups have initially concentrated in suburban residential areas.

Looking back 100 years or so, there were a few working-class concentrations in elite railroad and streetcar suburbs in Chicago, Philadelphia,

137

and New York. Many of their residents were municipal employees of the suburbs, and they worked grading streets and digging ditches.[1] However, the laborers' sections of these elite suburbs generally lacked enclave qualities. In the outer, or fringe, sections of several other cities, there were working-class communities that more closely resembled enclaves. In Jamaica Plain (outer Boston) around 1900, for example, factories opened near the same rail lines that had permitted Jamaica Plain to become an elegant area for wealthy Bostonians who worked in the center city. Many of the workers in these factories lived in the local community.[2] However, even though these communities were as enclave-like as most of the more elite "railroad suburbs," they were by definition not suburbs, because they were located within city limits. There were also some religious and life-style groups that established enclaves in the pristine countryside of upstate New York and southern Illinois; but because their places of settlement were not connected to any central city, they cannot qualify as suburban, either.

In contrast with earlier immigrants, who settled in inner cities, over the past twenty-five to thirty years many Asian American immigrants (or exiles) moved directly to the suburban areas of San Francisco and Los Angeles; Arab Americans left their homelands and immediately settled in the suburbs of Detroit and Washington; and Latin Americans moved to the suburbs of Miami and New York. And the communities they (and others) established in these undeniably suburban locations must generally be considered enclaves.

There are a number of reasons for this increase in suburban settlement. One is the differences in the kinds of people establishing the newer enclaves. For example, the relative wealth of many of the Taiwanese immigrants recently moving to metropolitan Los Angeles or the Filipinos moving to the San Francisco area has enabled them to settle in suburban areas that offer more amenities than the central cities.[3] Because of these recent trends, they can combine suburban and enclave living. For most of the earlier immigrants, the absence of suburban enclaves would have forced them to choose between life in an enclave and life in a suburb; but the choice was moot because few of them could afford to live in a suburb.

Prior to the last twenty-five to thirty years, most immigrant groups encouraged their members to "Americanize," while gay and other groups often tried to "pass." Moving up in the economic mainstream was assumed to require assimilation, or its outward appearance, and to involve geographical movement out of inner-city enclaves. However, this historical pattern of assimilation, upward mobility, and geographical movement outward was terminated by the arrival of wealthier exiles who established suburban enclaves. There is sufficient capital in these enclaves to permit people to be upwardly mobile without having to move out.

Furthermore, because businesspeople in a suburban enclave are frequently involved in extensive business dealings with their homelands, too much assimilation could entail economic disincentives. Refugees and their children have an advantage as entrepreneurs or employees because they share a culture and language with their counterparts in the native country. They may even be able to use family ties to build trust, a critical ingredient when business relationships are first established. For example, during the 1970s, many Vietnamese government officials and professionals fled the communists and settled south of Los Angeles, in an enclave that came to be called Little Saigon. Today, their children—American-trained lawyers, engineers, and bankers—are engaged in opening car rental agencies, hotels, and fast-food restaurants in Ho Chi Minh City (the former Saigon). In their visits to their parents' homeland, they learn or enhance their ability to speak Vietnamese, eat Vietnamese food, and participate in cultural observances. The result of these experiences is a further push away from assimilation.

Some of the older Vietnamese in Little Saigon are violently opposed to any dealings with the communists, and Vietnamese American businesspeople who travel to Vietnam or do business with the country have faced death threats. In this respect there are marked generational similarities between the Vietnamese in Little Saigon and the Cubans in Little Havana, as described in Chapter Six.[4]

Even when recent immigrant groups have not been markedly different from their predecessors, the establishment of enclaves in suburban locations has been encouraged by fundamental changes in cities and suburbs and their interrelationship. Specifically, some activities formerly concentrated in cities have been moved to suburbs. Most notable from our perspective are manufacturing jobs, which during the past thirty years or so have become increasingly located in suburban areas. These jobs have historically attracted immigrants (and other migrants) because they are high-paying entry-level jobs with limited educational requirements. As recent immigrants have settled close to where these jobs are now located, they have created enclaves that are very similar to those that previously tended to be confined to central cities.

One notable difference between many suburban enclaves at the turn of the twenty-first century and inner-city enclaves at the turn of the twentieth century concerns the contemporary merging of kindred racial and ethnic groups. Many of today's suburban enclaves are possible only because more encompassing social categories, such as "Asian" or "Latino," have evolved. In many suburbs, groups from some individual nations are too small to support separate, self-contained communities. Thus, an enclave can form only when there is solidarity among kindred groups. As an illustration, consider the differences between the near west side of the city of Chicago, circa 1910, and suburban Port Chester, New York, circa 1995. The center of the west side of Chicago contained a number of highly concentrated enclaves of Bohemians, Jews, and Italians, surrounded by those of Poles and Greeks.[5] Despite overlap and interpenetration of communities, it was possible to identify each ethnic group's own distinct enclaves. Each shopped at their own grocery stores, attended their own churches and synagogues, and attempted to avoid prolonged interaction with others. No shared conception of themselves as European Americans tied them together.

In contemporary Port Chester, in contrast, Latino immigrants pursuing the factory jobs that have moved to this suburb from New York and other cities have created a suburban enclave. Their countries of origin are varied, including El Salvador, Cuba, Puerto Rico, and Colombia. Members of each nationality group have "stretched" their culture to support the others' through such businesses as restaurants and groceries, *botánicas* selling folk herbs, and *discotecas* (music stores). They could, of course, emphasize the historical differences that have separated each from the others, rather than the similarities, such as their common language, food preferences, and liking for outdoor gatherings with loud music.[6] However, similarities are more likely to be emphasized in a society in which multiculturalism is valued.

Multiculturalism is, of course, a diffuse concept with many referents. One of the core ideas, however, involves opposition to the views of heterosexual, white, European males. People who are *other* than the preceding regard that group as having historically attempted to impose their world view on everyone else.[7] Groups comprising persons who are "other" have emphasized the authenticity of their own world views and unique heritages, and they have frequently tried to form inclusive intergroup coalitions in order to support each other. A poignant example of how far this "other" category can reach was provided in the Spike Lee film, *Do the Right Thing*, which examined relations among Italians, African Americans, Koreans, and others in a crowded inner-city neighborhood. In an angry confrontation with a crowd of African Americans, a frustrated Korean American shopkeeper shouts, "Please don't . . . I black . . . like you."[8]

FOOD AS METAPHOR

The life-styles and values of many distinctive groups are represented by their customary foods: what they choose, how it is prepared and eaten, and what foods they abstain from eating. Through their cuisine, people maintain traditions and group attachments. For example, many Southeast Asians working in American hotels will forgo a free meal at work and wait until they get home, to the company of others like themselves, to eat their own food purchased in Asian grocery stores. Sharing familiar food is the most frequently relied upon way for the Southeast Asians (and other groups) to "enjoy a sense of oneness."[9]

The epithets with which people have traditionally slurred members of various ethnic groups have also been drawn heavily from the foods and drinks associated with each. Thus, in examining the nicknames assigned to different groups, sociologist Irving L. Allen found many that were food related: "Potato heads" (Irish), "Spags" (Italians, from spaghetti), "Hop heads" (Germans), "Rice bellies" (Chinese), and so on.[10] Pejorative terms have also been made of foods and drinks associated with religious groups and life-style groups such as that of gays.

Focusing on food provides a convenient way to summarize the preceding discussion of multiculturalism and its effects on enclaves. Let us begin by noting that, in the past, the food preferences of various groups were both less likely to persist unchanged over time (because of pressures on group members to assimilate) and less likely to diffuse to members of other groups (because of weak multicultural ties among them). In Italian enclaves in Philadelphia, for example, traditional observance of Christmas Eve involved serving *baccalà* (salted cod), calamari, fried smelts, and broccoli.[11] From generation to generation, more traditionally American seafood and vegetables came to substitute for the traditional items; a declining proportion of Italians continued the holiday food tradition (either with the original or the modified menus); and relatively few non-Italians adopted the Italians' food ritual.

To illustrate the changes that have occurred in assimilation and multiculturalism, consider Jack Agueros, a Puerto Rican who grew up in Spanish Harlem in New York City. He writes about types of breads as metaphors for ethnic cultures. When he says that he wishes he could obtain the flaky, soft-crusted bread baked in Puerto Rico, I believe he means that he wants both the bread and an opportunity to immerse himself in Puerto Rican life. However, both the bread and Puerto Rico are three and one-half hours away by jet, so he settles for going to a nearby neighborhood where Puerto Ricans, Cubans, and Dominicans all make a very similar bread. Agueros writes that he hopes to retain his preference for authentic Puerto Rican bread, and not the Americanized version of it that is more readily available. His underlying fear is that he will move to a cultural and psychological middle ground, in which his identity will be diluted and lost: "not quite all Puerto Rican, not quite all American."[12]

Agueros described how, while growing up in New York, he also acquired a taste for many other types of ethnic breads, especially crusty Italian bread baked in the Italian section of East Harlem. It, too, can be difficult to obtain, though. The bread he now sees labeled as "Italian bread" in the mass chain supermarkets seems to him to be fit only to feed pigeons! Combining Italian bread with packaged American white bread, he says, has produced a watered-down product that is neither Italian nor American. He feels sorry for the people who are so assimilated that they like this bread. He is also sorry for those people whose one ethnic tie is so strong and pure that they can appreciate only one kind of bread.

LOCALIZATION

The development of specialized, local commercial and institutional activities within enclaves appears to run counter to one of the major trends in contemporary society, namely, the growth of the franchise: "chains" of stores offering a standard product regardless of where in the world they are located. Sociologist George Ritzer calls this trend the "McDonaldization" of contemporary society.[13] From fast-food restaurants to supermarkets, from motels to tourist agencies, Ritzer describes the rationality that has placed franchises offering standardized products across all of America, and the rest of the world as well. Each item is carefully weighed, packaged, priced, and sold in the most efficient manner. Most of all, the franchises offer predictability: the taste of a Big Mac, the room in a Holiday Inn, even the stores in a shopping mall will be the same in Pittsburgh as in Dallas and Portland.

Some people (including Ritzer and myself) regret that we live in a world in which franchises have transformed the different and exotic into the familiar and mundane. It also appears, though, that many people have come to value this "assembly-line" uniformity and predictability. In a poll taken by a local magazine, for example, residents of Roanoke, Virginia, selected Pizza Hut (and not some locally owned restaurant) as having the best pizza, and Kroger's (rather than some locally owned bakery) as having the best bread and pies.[14]

There is little doubt but that *McDonaldization* accurately describes a major trend in contemporary society. Even so, the impact of this trend on local communities should not be overstated. In some instances, communities have been able to keep out chains that they felt did not fit in. Thus, in Lincoln Park, an affluent, gentrified community on Chicago's lakefront, there was widespread objection to a proposed McDonald's. Some residents believed that a better class of restaurant belonged in the neighborhood. Others objected to McDonald's "suburban" appearance in a very urban setting. As a result of the actions of local community groups, the zoning variance requested by McDonald's was eventually denied by the Chicago City Council, and no McDonald's was erected. Then the same community groups assisted a restaurant that they believed better fit the neighborhood in moving into the proposed McDonald's location and obtaining a liquor license.[15]

When a community is an enclave, there is probably the greatest likelihood that national and international firms will adapt to the local area.

Thus, many chains have modified the standard architecture of their store and their local billboard advertisements to feature persons of the same race, ethnicity, or life-style as those who live in the surrounding enclave. Other illustrations of this phenomena include local branches of national travel agencies (and hotel chains) that offer singles-only, males-only, and other tours customized to fit the local area; and franchise restaurant menus and ATM instructions at bank branches that are written both in English and in the predominant foreign languages of the area. This "localization" of franchises results in commercial developments that reinforce the distinctiveness of enclaves. And although national chains are formidable competition, truly local restaurants, bookstores, groceries, night clubs, and the like continue to exist alongside both localized and national chains.

Similar forces bucking the standardization process are found in the institutional life of enclaves, as in schools, churches, and YMCAs. On the one hand are the truly local schools, associations, and clubs without links to outside organizations, whose mission is solely to serve local interests. On the other hand, there are local branches of national or citywide organizations. These exhibit not only the uniformity across communities that would be expected of branches that must answer to outside headquarters, but also the influence of their local enclaves in such aspects as the languages that are spoken, the kinds of support groups that are formed, and the types of specialized activities that are offered. The Bay Area United Way, for example, funds agencies in San Francisco that provide services to local gay populations. Other local chapters of United Way have included agencies associated with such institutions as local labor organizations and Jewish organizations. The only types of agencies generally excluded by United Ways, in fact, are those that receive national support precisely because they are not linked to a local community.[16]

In order to accomplish their tasks, local agencies attached to a city, state, or national organization must also interact with other local agencies (which may or may not be linked to other outside units). Hall describes how police and schools, for example, are typically parts of a network of interorganizational relations involving neighborhood citizen committees, local clinics, and neighborhood centers. Through these interorganizational relations, local groups influence local agencies.[17]

There has also been a burgeoning of specialized neighborhood communications, primarily consisting of newspapers that focus on (and are distributed within) particular enclaves. Modern technology has also made it possible to customize citywide communications media to local areas. Examples are provided by the special neighborhood sections that are selectively distributed inside of major daily newspapers in many cities, and local-access cable television programming in many cities that is customized to fit the interests of diverse local groups.

Finally, we note the opposite trend: specialized local programming that has itself become "franchised." For example, "Party Talk" is a syndicated gay talk show that appears on cable systems in Los Angeles, San Francisco, Chicago, Miami, and New York. Its host is Mr. Linda Simpson, a drag queen, and it features movie reviews by Cathay Che, an Asian American lesbian.[18] Serving as further illustration, "Arab-Net" is an Arabic language radio network that broadcasts in cities with large Arab American communities: Detroit, Chicago, Los Angeles, Pittsburgh, and Washington. It contains a mixture of local and network programming.[19] Thus, these broadcasts reflect a McDonaldization of enclaves, while simultaneously exhibiting the effects of localization.

NOTES

1. Kenneth T. Jackson, *Crabgrass Frontier,* New York: Oxford University Press, 1985.
2. Alexander von Hoffman, *Local Attachments,* Baltimore: Johns Hopkins University Press, 1994.
3. A majority of Asian Americans now live in suburbs, and their average family income in 1991 was over $56,000. See William P. O'Hare, William H. Frey, and Dan Foot, "Asians in the Suburbs," *American Demographics* 16, 1994.
4. For further discussion of the Vietnamese refugee group, see *The New York Times,* December 5, 1994, p. A8.
5. Natalie Walker, "Chicago Housing Conditions. X.," *American Journal of Sociology* 21, 1915.
6. For further discussion, see *The New York Times,* July 29, 1993, p. B4.
7. For further discussion of the polarities leading to cultural conflict in America, see James D. Hunter, *Culture Wars,* New York: Basic Books, 1991.
8. Quoted and discussed in Robert D. Manning, "Cultural Diversity or Diverse Cultures," *Proteus* 10, 1993.
9. Trans Minh Tung, "Southeast Asian Expatriates," in Ernest R. Myers (Ed.), *Challenges of a Changing America,* San Francisco: Austin & Winfield, 1994, p. 69.
10. Irving L. Allen, *The Language of Ethnic Conflict,* New York: Columbia University Press, 1983.
11. See Judith G. Goode et al., "Meal Formats, Meal Cycles and Menu Negotiation in the Maintenance of an Italian-American Community," in Mary Douglas (Ed.), *Food in the Social Order,* New York: Russell Sage Foundation, 1984.

12. Jack Agueros, "Beyond the Crust," in Kathleen Aguero (Ed.), *Daily Fare*, Athens: University of Georgia Press, 1993, p. 220.
13. George Ritzer, *The McDonaldization of Society*, Thousand Oaks, CA: Pine Forge Press, 1993.
14. *Roanoke Times and World News*, September 17, 1993. (I am indebted to George Ritzer for calling this item to my attention.)
15. Gerald D. Suttles, *The Man-Made City*, Chicago: University of Chicago Press, 1990, p. 81.
16. Deborah Kaplan Polivy, "The United Way," in Carl Milofsky (Ed.), *Community Organizations*, New York: Oxford University Press, 1988.
17. See Richard H. Hall, *Organizations: Structures, Processes, and Outcomes*, Englewood Cliffs, NJ: Prentice Hall, 1991. (See especially pp. 216–23.)
18. *The New York Times*, February 20, 1994, Section 9, p. 4.
19. Samia El-Badry, "The Arab-American Market," *American Demographics* 16, 1994.

Index

About the Author

M ark Abrahamson has been Professor of Sociology at the
University of Connecticut (Storrs) since 1976. During this period
he served for five years as head of the Department of Sociology
and for three and one-half years as the university's Associate Vice President
for Academic Affairs. He also spent two years on leave as Program Director
for Sociology at the National Science Foundation in Washington.

His continuing research and writing interests focus on urban poverty
and out-of-wedlock births. Professor Abrahamson has previously authored
eight books and over thirty articles published in professional journals and
anthologies.